Thirty Years at the Mansion

Liza inspects a formal setting in the main dining room. (Photo by Jerry Staley)

Thirty Years at the Mansion
Recipes and Recollections

Liza Ashley
as told to Carolyn Huber

Liza Ashley

5-13-91

August House / Little Rock
PUBLISHERS

Published 1985 by August House, Inc., P.O. Box 3223,
Little Rock, Arkansas, 72203, 501-372-5450

10 9 8 7 6 5 4

Library of Congress Catalog Card No. 84-73313
International Standard Book No. 0-935304-88-6 (HB)
International Standard Book No. 0-87483-135-0 (PB)

Project Editor: Liz Parkhurst
Design Director: Ted Parkhurst
Typography: Photo Type, Inc.
Cover Design and Production Artwork: Byron Taylor
Front Cover Photograph: Hubert Smith
Back Cover Photograph: Jerry Staley

Fourth Printing, 1991

(On the back cover)
A full place setting of the Governor's official china, silver and crystal. Mrs. McMath, whose husband was the first governor in the new Mansion, selected these patterns. (Photo by Jerry Staley)

To Carolyn Huber.
We will never find another one like her.

With best wishes,
Carolyn Huber

*This sterling silver punchbowl comes from the **U.S.S. Arkansas** and was made from 3,000 silver dollars donated by schoolchildren throughout Arkansas in 1913. (Photo by Jerry Staley)*

Contents

Introduction

Eliza Jane Ashley is an historical figure. She has lived among and influenced generations of Arkansas leaders for thirty years. She has been at the center of electoral victory and defeat, moral and political crises, personal triumphs and travails. She has met presidents, movie stars and millionaires. She has cooked for and eaten with politicians of every ideology. She has listened to and counseled with governors and their families and staff. Her years of service at the Governor's Mansion have left their mark on history.

Equally important, however, is another reason why Mrs. Ashley merits her place in history. Even if chance had never brought her to her position, she has lived her life with strength of character, common sense and devotion to hard work and to her religious faith that represents the best Arkansas has to offer.

Liza Ashley is also a very good cook. For three decades she has caused governors and their families to fight and lose battles of the bulge. It is high time that she shared her famous recipes with a wider audience.

The pages that follow are filled with both recipes and reminiscences of a remarkable woman, an Arkansas treasure, and our good friend Liza Ashley.

Bill, Hillary and Chelsea Clinton

Liza and Marilyn Blann prepare for the American Bar Association Dinner, 1977.

*Liza with first lady Nancy Reagan and the Whites at the Little Rock Airport.
(Courtesy the White House)*

First lady Rosalynn Carter greets Liza as Emma Phillips and Rosie Spann look on. (Courtesy the White House)

Mrs. Cherry, with her daughter, Charlotte, making a gift of a grandfather clock to the Mansion during Governor Pryor's tenure.

Visiting the Arkansas Governor's Mansion August 5, 1977, actor Gregory Peck pauses for a picture with (from left) Liza, Emma Phillips and Rosie Spann.

Liza with Barbara Bush, wife of Vice President George Bush.

Winthrop Paul Rockefeller pauses with Liza in front of the range he donated to the Mansion.

Foreword

Liza Ashley was born on the Oldham Plantation in Pettus (Lonoke County), Arkansas, on October 11, 1917. Even at birth, Liza was in contact with the chief executive of the State of Arkansas. W.K. Oldham, Sr., the owner of the plantation and her future employer, was a brother-in-law of former Governor James P. Eagle. (And later, Liza would work for Governor Eagle's niece, Mrs. Bessie Eagle Dunaway, in Little Rock.)

From the time she was born until she got big enough to work, Liza went to the Oldhams' house every day with her grandmother. When she was fifteen years old, Mrs. Oldham made her a cook, as her grandmother was. So Liza has been cooking all her life, though some things about it have changed. Back then, for example, they cooked on a woodstove; today Liza cooks on a commercial gas stove that was given to the Governor's Mansion by Winthrop Paul Rockefeller, son of former Governor Winthrop Rockefeller.

Mr. Oldham had come to Arkansas from Kentucky, and he liked fried cornbread, so Liza made cornbread 365 days a year — They called it "hot water cornbread." Liza went to work every morning at 6:00 o'clock and worked all day, through the dinner meal. At first, she cooked, cleaned, washed and ironed, but finally the Oldhams saw that this was too much for her to do and got someone to help. One of the biggest problems, according to Liza, was that she could never sweep the porch to the Oldhams' satisfaction. The house was two stories tall with a wrap-around porch and was situated on a dusty road. Even with regular sweeping, it never did stay clean, because as soon as the next car went by, it stirred up the dust and got it all over the porch again.

When and where Liza was growing up, children attended one-room schools and most of the teachers were eighth-grade graduates. Liza only went to school about three months out of the year because of all the farm work that had to be done. Liza remembers going to the cotton gin with her grandfather and riding on the press.

If formal education was hard to come by, entertainment was simple. Liza had a radio that was operated by electricity that she ran to her house from the Oldhams'. Everyone from miles and miles around would come to listen to "Amos & Andy" and Joe Louis fights.

Everyone's eating habits were different then, too. Liza's family would bring lard sandwiches — created by putting lard between two biscuits — in their school lunches. When they ran out of flour for biscuits, they ate cornbread with sorghum.

In 1942, Liza left the Oldham Plantation, even though the Oldhams warned her, "Oh, Liza, you'll never make it on your own." She went to work at the arsenal plant in Jacksonville for a short while and then for Mrs. Dunaway in Little Rock. After World War II, she went back to cooking and cleaning for different families in Little Rock's fashionable Pulaski Heights area. In 1952, she went to El Paso, Texas, where she worked briefly at Texas Western College.

The next year, 1953, Liza returned to Little Rock, and a year after that went to work as a maid at the Governor's Mansion. Francis Cherry was governor then, only the second to live in the Mansion, which had been completed in 1950. Henry Scribner was cook at the time. Liza worked under the supervision of his wife, Georgia, and filled in for Rev. Scribner as cook on his days off. When Mrs. Scribner resigned, Liza took her position.

When Orval Faubus became governor in 1955, his wife, Alta, wanted a woman cook. It was then that Liza became the cook at the Governor's Mansion, a position she has held for thirty years now. To my knowledge, she has the longest tenure of any cook at any Governor's Mansion in the country.

Liza has served seven governors: Cherry, Faubus, Rockefeller, Bumpers, Pryor, Clinton, White, and Clinton again. She has nothing but kind words about the families she has worked for in the Mansion. When pressed to name a favorite, she replies with utmost sincerity, "Now you know they were all my families. I don't have favorites. I liked them all, and they were all nice to me."

She is equally diplomatic about her political inclinations. When asked whether she is a Democrat or a Republican, she just grins and says, "I'm an Arkansan. I always vote for who I work for, for the governor at the time."

Liza is married to Fred Ashley and is very active in Canaan Missionary Baptist Church in Little Rock. She has one son, Louis Calvin Dodson, who "grew up in the mansion. I can still see him everywhere." Louis lives in Los Angeles and has two children, Elgin David and Chanel Monique.

Carolyn Huber

Little Rock, Arkansas
March, 1985

Governor Francis A. Cherry, Arkansas's thirty-fifth governor. (Photo by Fox Art Shop, Jonesboro, courtesy Mrs. Francis Cherry)

Governor Francis Cherry
1953–1954

In 1954, Mrs. Georgia Scribner, who was a maid at the Governor's Mansion, asked me to apply for work there. I came to the Governor's Mansion in September, 1954, when the Cherrys were serving their second year in the Mansion. Mrs. Scribner's husband, Henry, was the cook, and I did not do any cooking for the Cherrys except on his day off. I worked as a maid.

Governor and Mrs. Cherry had three children, Scott, Charlotte and Francis, Jr. When they were living in the Mansion, the state did not appropriate very much money for the governor to decorate the Mansion or purchase groceries — I believe it was about $12,000 — so they had to pay for their own entertaining back then. The staff was so small that Governor Cherry drove himself to the Capitol and back every day.

Mrs. Cherry did have a secretary, which Mrs. McMath had not. Her secretary was Edith Johnson. Mrs. Cherry spent a lot of time singing and cutting ribbons, and I didn't get to see her too much. Many years later, in 1976, Mrs. Cherry presented the Mansion with a grandfather clock made about 1770 in Waterford, Ireland, in memory of her husband.

As the following recipes show, the Cherrys liked just plain Southern cooking.

Liza's Fried Chicken

Cut up 1 large fryer. Salt and pepper and marinate pieces in sweet milk for 1 to 1½ hours. Roll in flour and fry in Crisco in an iron skillet.

(Everyone loves Liza's fried chicken, and she serves it often for Southern dinners.)

Rice Pilaf

1	stick butter, melted
1	medium-sized chopped onion
2	cups uncooked rice
2	cans beef consomme
1	can cream of mushroom soup

Melt butter in a large pan. Saute onion and rice until brown. Add consomme and mushroom soup and bring to boil. Pour in baking dish and bake, covered, at 350°. After 15 minutes, stir to keep rice from settling to bottom. Continue baking for 15 minutes more.

This has been served at a lot of buffet dinners. Liza tries to serve lots of rice in the Mansion, since Arkansas is one of the leading exporters of rice.

Garlic Grits

1	cup grits
1	package garlic cheese, shredded
¼	pound Cheddar cheese, shredded
1	stick butter
3	dashes Worcestershire sauce
3	egg whites, stiffly beaten

Cook grits. Add shredded cheese, butter, and Worcestershire. Set aside. Just before ready to bake, add egg whites. Bake about 30 minutes in a 350° oven.

This is a good recipe to serve at buffets and a good alternative to potatoes or rice with roast beef.

Chicken Vegetable Soup

1	fryer, boiled
6	cups water
1	bay leaf
1	onion, chopped
3	stalks celery
2	teaspoons salt
½	teaspoon pepper
½	cup rice
1	cup diced carrots
1	6-ounce package spaghetti

In a large pot, combine chicken, water, bay leaf, onion, celery, salt and pepper. Bring to boiling. Cover and simmer for 1½ hours or until tender. Remove chicken from broth; cool and remove meat from bones. Cut chicken into bite-sized pieces and set aside.

Skim excess fat from broth. Discard bay leaf. Bring broth to a boil and add rice, carrots and spaghetti. Cover and simmer until spaghetti is cooked. Add chicken and heat through for 10 to 15 minutes. Season with salt and pepper.

Yields 8 servings.

Bean Casserole

1	can French-cut string beans, drained
1	can sliced water chestnuts, drained
1	can English peas, drained
1	large onion
1	can cream of mushroom soup
1	small can Pet Milk
	sharp Cheddar cheese, grated
	bread crumbs

Grease casserole. Slice and cook onion until tender. Arrange ingredients in layers in order given above, using half of each ingredient (except bread crumbs) in sequence and then the other half again. Top with bread crumbs. Bake at 325° until casserole is bubbly and is thoroughly hot.

Governor Cherry receives election congratulations and a hug from his fondest supporter. (Courtesy Old State House Museum)

Angel Biscuits

4	cups flour
2	cups buttermilk
1	tablespoon sugar
2	teaspoons salt
1	teaspoon soda
3	teaspoons baking powder
1	cup shortening
1	package dry yeast, dissolved in a little warm water

Mix 2 cups of flour with remaining ingredients with an electric mixer. Then mix in remainder of flour. Knead, adding flour if necessary. Let rise 45 minutes, then punch down. Refrigerate and use as needed. Cut into desired shape and bake at 450° for 10 or 15 minutes.

Governor-elect and Mrs. Cherry are joined by campaign workers in a victory salute. (Courtesy Old State House Museum)

Pecan Pie

3	eggs, beaten
2/3	cup sugar
1/3	teaspoon salt
1/3	cup melted butter
1	cup dark corn syrup
1	unbaked 9-inch pie shell
1	cup pecan halves

Combine eggs, sugar, salt, butter and corn syrup in a medium-sized bowl and mix well. Pour mixture into pie shell and top with pecan halves. Bake at 375° for 45 minutes.

Fresh Apple Cake

2	eggs
1	cup oil
2	cups sugar
3	cups flour
2	teaspoons cinnamon
2	teaspoons soda
2	teaspoons salt
3	cups diced apples
1/2	cup nuts

Beat eggs, stir in oil, then sugar. Sift flour, cinnamon, soda and salt, and slowly add to egg mixture. Stir in apples and nuts. Bake at 350° for about 40 minutes or until knife comes out clean.

Sweet Potato Casserole

6½	cups cooked and mashed sweet potatoes
1½	cups brown sugar
3	eggs
¼	teaspoon ginger
¼	teaspoon allspice
½	teaspoon cinnamon
½	teaspoon nutmeg
½	teaspoon vanilla
1½	13-ounce cans Pet Milk
1	stick butter, melted
1	package salad marshmallows

Mix all ingredients except for marshmallows. Top mixture with marshmallows and bake at 400° for 30-40 minutes.

This recipe has been served to all the governors. If you have trouble with it, call Liza. After she had made it over the years with a pinch here and a pinch there, it was hard for us to get it down on paper.

Lemon Cheese Tarts

6	tart shells
1	8-ounce package Philadelphia cream cheese
2	eggs
½	cup sugar
3	tablespoons lemon juice (use 4 for more tartness)
1	cup whipping cream
2	tablespoons confectioners' sugar
1	teaspoon vanilla

Soften cheese and whip until fluffy. Add eggs, one at a time, beating after each. Blend in sugar and juice. Pour into tart shells. Bake at 350° for 15 to 20 minutes, until slightly firm. Chill and top with whipping cream sweetened with sugar and vanilla.

These are delicious garnished with fresh strawberries.

Chow-Chow

2	quarts finely chopped cabbage
6	medium onions, chopped
6	green peppers, coarsely chopped
6	red peppers, coarsely chopped
1	quart peeled, chopped green tomatoes
¼	cup pickling salt
6	cups vinegar (5% acidity), divided
2	tablespoons prepared mustard
2½	cups sugar
2	tablespoons mustard seed
1	tablespoon mixed pickling spices
1½	teaspoons ground turmeric
1	teaspoon ground ginger

Combine vegetables and salt; stir well. Cover and let stand 8 to 10 hours or overnight. Drain well.

Stir 2 tablespoons vinegar into mustard. Combine mustard mixture with remaining vinegar, sugar, mustard seeds, pickling spices, turmeric and ginger in a large kettle. Bring to a boil; reduce heat and simmer 20 minutes. Add vegetables; simmer an additional 10 minutes.

Pack solidly into pint jars, leaving headspace of ¼ inch. Cover at once with metal lids and screw bands tight. Process in boiling water bath for 10 minutes.

Yields 10 pints.

Cranberry Salad

1	package gelatin
1	cup + 3 tablespoons water
1	package lemon Jello
1	16-ounce can whole cranberry sauce
	rind from 1 orange, grated
	juice from 1 orange
3½	tablespoons lemon juice

Soften gelatin in 3 tablespoons cold water. Boil 1 cup water and dissolve lemon Jello. Mix in softened gelatin. Add all other ingredients and mix well. Chill.

Yields 6 servings.

Governor Cherry, Mrs. Cherry and their children, Francis, Jr., Charlotte and Scott. (Courtesy Mrs. Francis Cherry)

Governor and Mrs. Faubus at the Capitol on inauguration day, 1963. (Courtesy Governor's Office)

Governor Orval E. Faubus
1955–1966

In January, 1955, we had a change in governors. Orval Faubus had been elected, and he and his wife, Alta, and their son, Farrell, moved to the Mansion from Huntsville. He served twelve years.

When Mrs. Faubus moved in, she did not want a man to do the cooking. She wanted a woman. She asked me to be the cook, but I hated to take the job because Henry was my friend. Mrs. Faubus said, "Well, if you don't take it, somebody else will," so that's how I became cook at the Governor's Mansion.

Since the state did not appropriate the funds to hire enough help, the Faubuses brought in prisoners from Cummins to help in the kitchen and the yard. In addition to the inmates, some of my helpers were Mary Paxton, Johnnie Hart and Elijah Gordon. Since Mrs. Faubus did not have very much experience in cooking and running a household, I did most of the planning of the meals. Calvin

Shackleford would come in and help out, too, when we needed him. We worked six days a week and never had Sundays off. There was always lots of entertaining. We also worked all the holidays because the Faubuses always had lots of company.

In 1957, when the integration crisis started, it was really hard on us. Governor and Mrs. Faubus were attending the Southern Governors' Conference in Sea Island, Georgia, and they were called back to Little

A dinner party scene during the Faubus years. (Courtesy Governor's Office)

Rock. The Mansion staff had been off, and we were all called back in. I watched out the window and saw the federal people come and serve the warrant on Governor Faubus. Then President Eisenhower sent in troops to shield the nine black students that were attending Central High School. We worked long hours. There were people going and coming all the time, and we really had a lot of people to feed through the crisis.

Farrell was not treated well at Central High by the other students, so he went back to Huntsville to finish high school. Later he married Martha Jo and they lived in Little Rock. They had two little girls, Fara Elizabeth (Governor Faubus had said if the baby was a girl, he was going to try to get Liza in her name some way, and that's how she got the name Elizabeth) and Ellen.

The Faubuses loved Southern cooking and thoroughly enjoyed any meal that featured green beans, blackeyed peas and cornbread. He also loved chicken and dumplings and roast beef, best of all he loved my pound cake. I kept one baked for him all the time. We also cooked lots of quail, duck, deer and other game that people would send us.

Mrs. Dixie Cain came down from Huntsville to serve as secretary to Mrs. Faubus, and she helped me run the Mansion. We had some interesting guests during that time such as Governor John Connally of Texas and his wife, Nellie. They seemed so nice. They would come back to the kitchen and talk to us. Also, former President Harry Truman spent a night in the guesthouse in 1958. He was in Little Rock for the 35th Division Association reunion.

In 1961, while the Faubuses were still here, the Mansion had its first complete redecorating. They hired Elvis Presley's decorator, George Golden of Memphis. I think the whole thing cost $7,000.

One day, Governor Faubus told me, "Liza, I'm going home, I'm going to retire." He didn't want to, but he felt like Mrs. Faubus was unhappy and Farrell wanted him to leave. This ended our twelve years together. It had been just like a family. Faubus never talked much, he just liked to sit back in the kitchen and eat pound cake. Mrs. Faubus and I became close friends over those twelve years, and we still correspond today.

Old-Fashioned Chicken Pie

1	stewing chicken
3	cups water
1	medium onion, peeled and sliced
1	handful celery tops
1	teaspoon salt
¼	teaspoon pepper
1	bay leaf
½	cup flour
1⅔	cups undiluted evaporated milk
2	cups cooked, sliced carrots
1	pound small white onions, cooked
6	baking powder biscuits, uncooked (recipe follows)

Place chicken in large kettle with water, onion, celery, salt, pepper and bay leaf. Simmer 1½ to 2 hours or until tender. Remove chicken from broth; strain broth and cool. Remove chicken from bones, leaving it in rather large pieces. Skim fat from broth; measure out ½ cup of fat and 2⅓ cups of broth.

Heat the ½ cup fat in a large saucepan. Blend in flour; stir in the 2⅓ cups broth and evaporated milk. Cook, stirring constantly, until the sauce thickens. Boil 1 minute.

Add chicken, carrots and onions, and salt and pepper if needed. Reheat. Pour into a 3-quart baking dish, and arrange biscuits over top. Bake at 450° for 20 or 25 minutes.

Liza first made this recipe for the Faubuses and has continued to make it for all the governors.

Watergate Salad

1	medium can crushed pineapple
1	can mandarin oranges
1	medium carton small-curd cottage cheese
1	box pistachio Jello instant pudding
½	cup small marshmallows
1	carton Cool Whip

Mix pineapple, mandarin oranges and cottage cheese. Add pudding mix and stir well. Add marshmallows and mix; finally, stir in Cool Whip.

This recipe was given to Liza by Alta Faubus, who says she serves this as a dessert as well as a salad.

Governor and Mrs. Faubus with Mansion personnel: (left to right) Elijah Gordon, Calvin Shackleford, Liza, the Faubuses, Leon Jefferson and York Wilborn.

Chicken Casserole

6	chicken breasts, deboned
6	pieces bacon, uncooked
1	jar chipped beef
1	can cream of mushroom soup
1	pint sour cream

Roll one piece of bacon around each chicken breast, securing with a toothpick. Line casserole with chipped beef. Place chicken rolls in casserole. Mix soup and sour cream and pour over chicken. Bake uncovered at 250° for 3 hours.

Exotic Turkey Salad

2	quarts coarsely cut cooked white turkey meat
1	20-ounce can sliced water chestnuts
2	pounds seedless green grapes
2	cups toasted slivered almonds
3	cups mayonnaise
1	tablespoon curry powder
2	tablespoons soy sauce
1	can pineapple chunks, with juice

Mix all ingredients except ½ cup almonds and pineapple. Chill. Just before serving, add the pineapple and toss lightly. Serve in nests of Bibb lettuce. Garnish with remaining almonds.

Yields 12 servings.

Faubus Fruit Fluff

2	pounds red grapes, seeded
1	Number 303 can crushed pineapple
1	package salad marshmallows
1	cup chopped pecans
1	package plain gelatin
3	egg yolks
	juice of 3 lemons
½	cup sugar
1	pint whipping cream

Mix grapes, pineapple, marshmallows and pecans. Sprinkle lightly with gelatin and set aside. Combine egg yolks, lemon juice and sugar in a saucepan and cook until thick. Cool completely, then mix with fruit. Fold in whipping cream and chill.

Liza serves this for the governors at Thanksgiving and Christmas dinners.

Black Cherry Salad

2	cans pitted black cherries
2	3-ounce packages Black Cherry Jello
1	envelope plain gelatin
2	tablespoons lemon juice
⅔	cup dry sherry

Drain cherries, reserving liquid, and set aside. Dissolve Jello and gelatin in 1 cup boiling water. Add lemon juice, cherry juice and water to equal 2 cups. Add sherry. Pour into 9-inch square pan. Add cherries and refrigerate until firm.

Yields 9 servings.

German Slaw

1	large cabbage, chopped
3	onions, slices
¾	cup sugar
1	teaspoon celery seed or celery salt
1	teaspoon dry mustard
1	teaspoon salt
1	cup apple cider vinegar
1	cup Wesson oil

Arrange cabbage and onions in bowl. Bring to a boil sugar, celery seed, mustard, salt and vinegar; add oil. Pour over cabbage and onion; chill for several hours. This will keep for up to three weeks.

This slaw is made and left for the governor and his family to eat on weekends.

Sesame Baked Chicken Breasts

14	large chicken breasts, boned and skinned
6	eggs, slightly beaten
3	tablespoons water
3	tablespoons soy sauce
¾	teaspoon pepper
¾	cup flour
1½	cups sesame seeds
1½	cups margarine

Blend eggs, water, soy sauce and pepper in a shallow dish. Dip each chicken in first flour, then egg mixture. Sprinkle heavily with sesame seeds. Melt margarine in baking pan. Add chicken and turn to coat with butter. Bake at 400° until golden brown and tender, about 40 to 50 minutes.

The mushroom sauce which follows is a delicious addition to this dish.

Mushroom Sauce

1	pound fresh mushrooms, sliced
½	cup margarine
½	cup flour
2	10-ounce cans condensed beef bouillon
½	cup heavy cream
4	tablespoons chopped parsley
	dash pepper

Saute mushrooms until golden. Cover and let simmer for 5 minutes. Blend in flour; add bouillon slowly, stirring until smooth. Stir in cream, parsley and pepper. Heat until just simmering.

Yields about 6 cups.

Chicken Divine

2	10-ounce packages frozen broccoli spears
3	cups cooked chopped chicken
2	cans cream of chicken soup
1	cup mayonnaise
1	tablespoon lemon juice
1	cup grated sharp Cheddar cheese
1	cup buttered bread crumbs

Grease casserole dish. Cook broccoli; drain and place in bottom of casserole. Place chicken over broccoli.

Mix soup, mayonnaise and lemon juice; pour over chicken. Cover with grated cheese. Top with bread crumbs.

Bake at 350° for 30 to 40 minutes.

This recipe was given to Liza by Alta Faubus, who got it from Christine Tucker of Benton.

Pound Cake

1	pound butter
3	cups sugar
6	eggs
3½	cups flour
1	teaspoon vanilla
1	cup buttermilk

Grease and flour tube pan. Cream butter and sugar well. Add eggs one at a time, beating well after each one. Then add the dry ingredients one at a time, mixing in a third of the buttermilk after each one. Bake in tube pan at 350° for 1 hour and 25 minutes.

This was Governor Faubus's favorite dessert, and it is also Governor Clinton's and Chelsea Clinton's favorite. Chelsea recommends topping it with vanilla ice cream.

Baked Beans

2	16-ounce cans Campbell's pork and beans
1	cup light brown sugar
2	tablespoons dry mustard
6	slices bacon, uncooked and cut in pieces
¾	cup catsup

Empty one can pork and beans into a greased casserole. Combine brown sugar and dry mustard; sprinkle half of this mixture over beans. Top with remaining can of beans. Layer with rest of sugar mixture, chopped bacon and catsup. Bake uncovered at 325° for 2 hours.

Never-Fail Hot Rolls

2	packages dry yeast
1½	teaspoon salt
¼	cup sugar
2	cups warm water
2	eggs, beaten
¼	cup oleo, melted
6½	cups all-purpose flour

Dissolve yeast, salt and sugar in warm water in large mixing bowl. Add eggs and oleo. Beat in 6½ cups flour (or more, depending on desired consistency). Knead a short time.

Place dough into large, greased mixing bowl. Cover with wax paper and place a wet cloth on top. Let set in warm place until it has doubled in bulk.

Punch down. Shape rolls as you wish. Put into a greased pan and let rise (allow about 2 hours). Bake at 350° for 15 minutes.

This recipe was given to Liza by Alta Faubus.

Liza and Willie Walton inspect a Hope watermelon

Strawberry Pie

1	9-inch baked pie shell
1	cup sugar
3½	tablespoons cornstarch
⅛	teaspoon salt
1	cup crushed strawberries
¼	cup oleo
¼	cup water
3	ounces cream cheese, softened
1	cup whole strawberries
1	cup whipping cream
¼	teaspoon almond extract
2	tablespoons powdered sugar

Combine sugar, cornstarch, salt, crushed strawberries, oleo and water in saucepan. Cook until thick and transparent. Cool.

Spread cream cheese over inside of pie shell. Stand whole strawberries in cream cheese. Spread cooled sauce over berries.

Whip cream; add almond extract and powdered sugar. Mix well and spoon onto pie. Chill.

This recipe was given to Liza by Alta Faubus.

Green Bean Casserole

1	can French-style green beans
1	can water chestnuts
1	large onion, chopped and cooked
1	can English peas
1	can cream of mushroom soup
1	small can Pet Milk
	sharp Cheddar cheese, grated
	buttered bread crumbs

Grease casserole dish; layer ingredients in dish in order given (except cheese and bread crumbs), making two series of layers. Top with grated cheese, then bread crumbs. Bake at 350° about 40 minutes.

Yields 6 servings.

Old-Time Buttermilk Pie

½	cup butter
2	cups sugar
3	rounded tablespoons flour
3	eggs, beaten
1	cup buttermilk
1	teaspoon vanilla
	dash nutmeg (optional)
1	9-inch unbaked pie shell

Let butter soften. Add sugar to butter and cream together well. Add flour and eggs; beat well. Stir in buttermilk, vanilla and nutmeg. Pour into unbaked pie shell. Bake for 45 to 50 minutes at 350°. Place on wire rack to cool completely before serving.

Liza's String Beans

4	pounds stringless pole beans
½	pound salt pork
	salt, to taste
1	tablespoon sugar
¼	teaspoon garlic salt
	dash of Beau Mode seasoning

Wash beans well, while boiling salt pork for 15 minutes. Add beans and seasonings. Cover and cook over medium-low heat for one hour.

This was one of Governor Faubus's favorite dishes when he was in the Mansion.

Baking Powder Biscuits

2	cups all-purpose flour
1	tablespoon + 1 teaspoon baking powder
½	teaspoon salt
¼	cup + 1 tablespoon shortening
¾	cup milk

Combine flour, baking powder and salt; stir well. Cut in shortening until mixture resembles coarse meal. Sprinkle milk evenly over flour mixture, stirring until dry ingredients are moistened. Turn dough out on a lightly floured surface; knead lightly 10 to 12 times. Roll dough to ½-inch thickness; cut with a 2¾-inch biscuit cutter. Place biscuits on a lightly greased baking sheet. Bake at 450° for 12 minutes or until lightly browned.

Yields 12 biscuits.

At his office in the State Capitol, March 21, 1966, Governor Faubus, after six terms as governor, announces his intention not to seek reelection.

Liza and Mrs. Faubus survey a catch of bass brought in by Governor Faubus, Wayne Hampton and party. (Courtesy Governor's Office)

Governor and Mrs. Faubus in costume for a masquerade ball. (Courtesy Governor's Office)

Governor Rockefeller takes his legislative program to the people. (Courtesy Estate of Winthrop Rockefeller)

Governor Winthrop Rockefeller
1967–1970

In January, 1967, Winthrop Rockefeller became governor. He did not move to the Mansion right away. He moved to a penthouse at the top of the National Old Line Building while the Mansion underwent renovation. Everything was moved out. They redid the downstairs by having oak floors put in the dining room, living room and east conference room. Then they purchased the oriental rugs that are in the living and dining rooms now. The foyer was covered with marble from Batesville. They repaired the wiring, the plumbing and the drainage; they finished off the basement and put in public restrooms. The Mansion really was in bad shape. There was an article in the *New York Times* about it, and Governor Rockefeller was quoted as saying, "Orval Faubus never let the fire marshal in the house. He was afraid the marshal might evict him."

I was very proud to have the kitchen completely redone with new cabinets. They moved the laundry room to the basement, which made the kitchen larger. I did not cook for the Rockefellers much, though, because they brought in their own cook, Ben Mitchell. I was his assistant, and I felt like I was getting a diploma. It was like going back to school, like it was a course in gourmet cooking.

The Rockefellers didn't eat the same kind of food that Southern people eat. They just didn't ever cook greens or peas for him. He liked creamed chicken and artichokes. First time I ever heard of artichokes was when the Rockefellers lived here. That gentleman could eat a million of them, and they had to be arranged so pretty on the plate.

Governor Rockefeller loved soup, and I was introduced to French onion soup, mushroom soup and vichyssoise. They had lamb and capon that came in from New York. Gone were the cornbread, the blackeyed peas and the green beans. One day we served quiche, and one of the guests said, "Why are we eating our pie first?" There was a lot of difference between Northern and Southern cooking.

Governor Rockefeller had one son, Winthrop Paul. Mrs. Rockefeller had two children, Anne and Bruce Bartley; they did not move into the Mansion with the Rockefellers. They were all very private people. When they did their own entertaining, they went to Winrock Farm up on Petit Jean Mountain. One exception was Senator Jay Rockefeller, who visited the governor here at the Mansion; of course, he was just a college student then.

Even though he didn't do much personal entertaining there himself, Governor Rockefeller let the people of the state have lots of parties at the Mansion. He let them enjoy it, because they were taxpayers and he thought they had a right to use the Mansion and the yard. He furnished everything; he was the only governor who was able to furnish all the food and flowers for entertaining. He would bring dishes and tables and chairs from his home on Petit Jean Mountain and put up tents for people to have their lawn parties in, and they would have teas and dinners for the garden club. Their chef, Ben, would fix those dinners up on the farm, and then they were brought down here.

Governor Rockefeller died in 1973. Governor Bumpers was in the Mansion then, and I went with him and his family to the funeral.

Artichokes — Rockefeller style

To cook, cut the tips of the leaves and most of the stem off; place upright in several inches of boiling water. Simmer for 30 to 45 minutes; drain upside down. For fancy serving, remove the choke or thistle portion with a spoon.

To eat, dip the tip of each leaf into a sauce and draw the end through your front teeth. Then discard the rest of the leaf. The bottom of the artichoke (the heart) is the best part. (Remember, don't eat the fuzzy choke above the heart.)

Serve with hollandaise or lemon-butter sauce.

Lobster Newburg

6	lobster tails, cooked and diced
1½	pints whipping cream
1	cup grated aged Cheddar cheese
1	teaspoon chicken base
¼	cup V-8 juice
3	tablespoons cooking sherry
1	dash red pepper
2	tablespoons cornstarch

Bring cream to boil. Add cheese, chicken base, V-8 juice, sherry and red pepper; stir well. Thicken with cornstarch. Add diced lobster tails. Bake at 350° for 20 minutes.

This recipe was given to Liza by Ollie Maxfield, chef at Winrock Farm, who recommends serving this over rice.

Broccoli Souffle

1	package frozen broccoli stalks
1	cup mayonnaise
1	cup mushroom soup
6	eggs
4	tablespoons grated sharp cheese
	salt and pepper to taste
	dash onion juice

Cook broccoli; drain thoroughly and cut in small pieces. Add mayonnaise and soup. Beat in eggs one at a time. Add cheese, salt, pepper and onion juice. Place in casserole dish; place dish in a pan of hot water. Bake at 350° for about 1 hour (begin checking after 45 minutes).

Cheese and Egg Souffle

8	slices bread
	butter
5	eggs
1	pint milk
½	Old English cheese, grated
	salt and pepper to taste

Butter baking dish. Trim crust from bread; butter each piece and cut into ½-inch cubes. Beat eggs and milk. Mix cheese and bread in baking dish. Pour egg mixture over cheese and bread. Let set 1 hour before cooking. Cook 45 minutes at 325° (or 30 minutes if using a glass baking dish).

Yields 10 servings.

Steak Marinade

1	bottle Wish Bone Italian Dressing
½	bottle Lea & Perrins Worcestershire Sauce
	ground peppercorns, to taste
⅛	tablespoon ground ginger
3	tablespoons bourbon

Mix ingredients together. Meat should be at room temperature and should marinate according to the thickness of the steak; but for best results it should not stay in marinade less than 4 hours.

This recipe can be made in large amounts and kept refrigerated to be used as needed.

This recipe is believed to belong to the Rockefeller family.

Vichyssoise

3	cups sliced potatoes
3	cups sliced white onions
	salt to taste
1½	quarts canned chicken broth
1	cup heavy cream
3	tablespoons minced chives

Simmer potatoes, onions and salt in chicken broth, partially covered, about 45 minutes or until vegetables are tender. Do not overcook. Puree soup in blender. Stir in cream. Taste for seasoning. Chill.

Serve in chilled soup cups and garnish with minced chives.

Yields 6 to 8 servings. Liza says this may be made ahead, but if you do this do not add cream until the last minute.

Cold Lemon Souffle

2	cups cold water
4	envelopes unflavored gelatin
16	eggs, separated
2	12-ounce cans frozen lemonade concentrate, defrosted
2	cups sugar
2	cups heavy cream, whipped

Place water in top of double boiler; sprinkle gelatin into the water to soften. Beat egg yolks lightly and add them to gelatin. Mix well. Place over boiling water and cook, stirring constantly, about 4 minutes or until gelatin dissolves and mixture thickens. Remove from heat and stir in lemonade concentrate. Chill until mixture thickens and drops from spoon in mounds.

Beat egg whites until stiff but not dry. Gradually beat in sugar and continue beating until egg whites are stiff. Fold whites into lemon mixture in large bowl. Fold in whipped cream.

Pour into individual serving bowls if possible or into a souffle dish with a wax paper collar. Refrigerate until firm. Just before serving, decorate with a little whipped cream.

Mrs. Rockefeller greets some very special guests on the back lawn of the Mansion.
(Courtesy UALR Library, Special Collections)

Great Clam Chowder

2	medium onions, diced
2	medium green peppers, diced
1	celery heart, diced
	butter
	thyme to taste
3	bay leaves
	salt and pepper to taste
½	cup clam juice
2	12-ounce bottles of beer
4	cups chopped clams
¼	cup half-and-half
1	teaspoon Worcestershire sauce
2	tablespoons sour cream

In large pan saute onion, pepper and celery in butter until tender. Add thyme, bay leaves, salt and pepper. Add clam juice, beer and chopped clams; bring to a boil. Add half-and-half and let simmer until chowder is consistency of cream.

Remove from heat and let sit for 20 minutes. Return to heat; add Worcestershire and blend in sour cream. Heat through but do not let come to a boil.

Governor and Mrs. Rockefeller at the Pink Tomato Festival in Warren. (Courtesy Estate of Winthrop Rockefeller)

Governor and Mrs. Rockefeller at the Republican National Convention, 1968. Rockefeller's campaign button reads, "Win Rockefeller for President: Arkansas' Favorite Son." (Courtesy Estate of Winthrop Rockefeller)

Cucumber and Mushroom Soup

3	cucumbers, peeled and thinly sliced
3½	tablespoons butter
2	small onions, chopped
1	pound fresh mushrooms, sliced
1	tablespoon flour
1	can good quality chicken broth
1	pint sour cream
5	mushrooms, sliced

Melt 3 tablespoons butter; add onions and cook over medium heat 2 to 3 minutes. Add mushrooms. Cover and cook until slightly tender. Add flour and rest of butter to thicken. Add chicken broth, then cucumbers, and simmer until cucumbers are transparent. Soup can be put away at this point.

To serve, add sour cream; mix and heat through. Top with a few sliced mushrooms.

Yields 6 servings.

Frozen Lemon Delight

1	graham cracker crust, baked in 9" x 13" pan
½	cup graham cracker crumbs
½	gallon vanilla ice cream, softened
1	6-ounce can lemonade concentrate, thawed

Mix ice cream and lemonade well and pour into cooled crust. Sprinkle with remaining crumbs and freeze.

Yields 12 large servings.

French Onion Soup

4	large onions
¼	cup butter
1	tablespoon flour
1½	quarts beef stock or consomme
12	toasted rounds of French bread
	Parmesan cheese

Peel and slice onions; separate rings. Heat butter in large saucepan. Add onion rings and cook them very, very gently over a low flame, stirring constantly with a wooden spoon until the rings are golden brown. Sprinkle with flour; when this has been well blended, gradually pour in beef stock or consomme (if consomme is used, follow directions on can). Stir constantly until soup begins to boil. Lower heat, cover pan and simmer for 30 minutes.

*Yields 12 servings. Liza says a nice addition to each serving is
a slice of round French bread toasted with a heaping of Parmesan cheese.*

Crab Quiche

1	unbaked pie shell
½	cup finely chopped onion
1	tablespoon butter
3	eggs, lightly beaten (for 8-inch pie shell; use 4 for 9-inch pie shell)
2	cups cream or half-and-half
1	teaspoon salt
½	pound Swiss cheese, finely grated
	dash nutmeg
	dash cayenne pepper
1	6½-ounce can lump crabmeat

Saute onion in butter for 5 minutes or until transparent. Set aside. Mix eggs, cream, salt, cheese, nutmeg and cayenne. Add onions and crabmeat. Pour into pie shell and bake at 450°; after 10 minutes, reduce heat to 325° and cook until done, 20 to 25 minutes.

This is also a favorite of Hillary Clinton's.

Chocolate Chiffon Pie

1	12-ounce can flaked coconut
1	cup butter
4	semi-sweet chocolate squares
1¼	cups sugar
4	eggs, separated
1	pinch salt
1	envelope unflavored gelatin
¼	cup cold water
1	teaspoon vanilla
	whipped cream

Brown coconut in ½ cup butter in skillet. Pat into 9-inch pie pan. Refrigerate 1 hour.

Melt chocolate in double boiler. Add ¾ cup sugar, egg yolks, salt and ½ cup butter. Cook until hot.

While chocolate mixture is cooking, dissolve gelatin in cold water. Add this mixture to chocolate; cook and stir 3 minutes. Let cool. Add vanilla.

Beat egg whites until stiff; add ½ cup sugar and fold into chocolate mixture. Pour into coconut crust and chill 1 hour.

Before serving, top with whipped cream.

This recipe was given to Liza by Ollie Maxfield.

Governor and Mrs. Rockefeller with the governor's brother David, chairman of the Chase Manhattan Bank, in front of the governor's Falcon Jet, which set several world speed records. (Courtesy Estate of Winthrop Rockefeller)

Mrs. Rockefeller, Lieutenant Governor Maurice "Footsie" Britt and Governor Rockefeller share the election limelight. (Courtesy Estate of Winthrop Rockefeller)

Governor and Mrs. Rockefeller share a quiet moment at their home atop Petit Jean Mountain. (Courtesy UALR Library, Special Collections)

Governor Bumpers and former Governor Rockefeller (Photo by W.L. "Pat" Patterson, courtesy **Arkansas Gazette***)*

Governor Dale Bumpers
1971–1974

In January, 1971, Governor Dale Bumpers, his wife Betty, and their children — Brent, Bill and Brooke — moved to the Mansion from Charleston.

Now it was back to cornbread, blackeyed peas and green beans again, for the Bumperses liked Southern cooking. I think the governor's favorite meal was pork chops, but he liked to eat everything. That man simply liked to eat. He liked my chicken and dumplings, and also raisin pie and carrot cake. It was because of the children that I started making my famous chocolate chip cookies.

Mrs. Bumpers didn't care anything about cooking and the kitchen. Her sister, Mrs. Ruth Wolfe of Fort Smith, came down and helped me get settled in. She helped me plan menus that they liked and gave me the recipes. I had two helpers. Mrs. Willie Mae Rollins was the upstairs maid, and Viola Clark was the downstairs maid. Mrs. Coleman came down from Charleston to help with Brooke and the boys. And we had Linda Miesner here to help out since Mrs. Bumpers could not keep up with all the secretarial work.

The Bumpers children were easy to get along with. They treated us with respect, and I became very attached to them. You could tell they had a good daddy behind them. The governor kept up with his boys. He waited up one night for Brent to come in, and after that, he didn't have any more trouble out of him. He told him that his mother and father were killed by somebody drinking, and he didn't intend for his boys to do that.

The Bumperses attended church every Sunday, and so for the first time, we had Sunday off so we could attend church, too. I attend Canaan Missionary Baptist Church, where I am supervisor of the Junior Ushers Board, and this meant a lot to me to be able to attend church.

Governor Bumpers was a great tennis player. He was the first person I had ever seen who came running through the kitchen putting his socks on as he went, trying to get to the courts to meet Mr. Ben Allen. He had a lot of fun playing tennis. He tried to watch his weight, but he loved to eat. He'd say "You're making me fat," and then as soon as he would get through eating, he'd go look in the icebox. I thought I was making him fat until I found out that he went to Fisher's in North Little Rock every Wednesday for lunch. That man loved to eat, period.

One night he was fixing to go to the movies and couldn't get anyone to go with him. He said, "Liza, do you want to go see a love story?" I said, "Sure, I want to go." So I pulled off my apron, and away we went.

While the Bumpers family was here, we got some new furnishings in the Mansion. (The Rockefellers had used a lot of their own furniture and then taken it with them when they left.) A cabinet was built for the silver from the *U.S.S. Arkansas*, and a chandelier was purchased that still hangs over the dining room table. We also got some living room furniture then. Mrs. Bumpers wanted to get me a new stove, but I near about cried, and she let me keep the one I had. This was during the energy crisis, too, and Governor Bumpers insisted on keeping the thermostat at 67 degrees.

I was glad to be in the kitchen then.

On December 20, 1974, Governor Bumpers proclaimed it "Eliza Jane Ashley Day" in a ceremony at the State Capitol. This was a great day for me, and he had a lot of pictures taken with me and then took me to lunch at Fisher's, one of his favorite places.

Governor Bumpers served two terms as governor and in 1974 ran for the United States Senate. He won and went to Washington and has been there ever since.

Liza's Famous Chocolate Chip Cookies

2	cups oleo or butter
1½	cups light brown sugar, packed
1½	cups sugar
2	teaspoons vanilla
2	tablespoons water
4	eggs
4	cups flour
2	teaspoons soda
1	teaspoon salt
2	cups nuts
2	12-ounce packages chocolate chips

Cream butter and sugars until light and fluffy. Add vanilla, water and eggs and beat well. Mix flour with soda and salt; blend into mixture. Stir in nuts and chocolate chips. Drop from teaspoon onto greased cookie sheet and bake at 350° for 8 to 10 minutes or until golden brown.

Yields about 8 dozen cookies.

Hash Brown Potato Casserole

1	32-ounce package shredded frozen potatoes
1	cup butter, melted and halved
1	can cream of chicken soup
12	ounces American cheese, grated
1	cup sour cream
1	teaspoon salt
½	small onion, chopped
1	cup cornflakes

Place thawed potatoes in 9" x 13" casserole. Mix ½ cup butter, soup, cheese, sour cream, salt and onion and pour over potatoes. Top with cornflakes mixed with ½ cup butter. Bake uncovered at 350° for 45 minutes.

Yields 12 to 15 servings. This is an especially good buffet dish.

Shrimp Snack

1	8-ounce package shrimp
2	tablespoons lemon juice
¼	cup diced celery
1	6-ounce package slivered almonds
⅓	cup mayonnaise
1	tablespoon chili sauce
	pinch dill weed

Boil shrimp; drain and add lemon juice. Mix other ingredients together and add to shrimp. Serve on lettuce bed.

This is a recipe you can make in a hurry if someone drops in unexpectedly. If you are really in a hurry, cool shrimp with ice cubes. Liza makes this sometimes on Friday before she leaves for the weekend.

Bumpers Chicken Casserole

9	slices white bread
9	slices sharp Cheddar cheese
4	cups cut-up chicken
½	pound fresh mushrooms
4	eggs
2	cups milk
1	can cream of mushroom soup
1	can cream of celery soup
1	can sliced pimentos

Grease casserole. Trim crusts off bread. Saute mushrooms in butter. Layer bread, cheese, chicken and mushrooms in casserole. Mix egg and milk, then pour into casserole. Beat soups together and stir in pimentos. Pour over top of casserole. Refrigerate overnight.

Bake in 350° oven for 50 minutes. Let stand 15 minutes before serving.

This was one of the Bumpers family's favorite dishes. It can also be made with turkey or tuna.

Carol's Carrot Cake

2	cups flour
2	cups sugar
3	cups grated carrots
2	teaspoons cinnamon
½	teaspoon salt
1	teaspoon baking powder
2	teaspoons baking soda
1½	cups oil
4	eggs
1	teaspoon vanilla

Mix all dry ingredients together. Add oil, eggs and vanilla and blend well. Bake in three nine-inch pans at 350° for 30 minutes or until done. Spread frosting (recipe follows) between layers and on top and sides of cake.

Carrot Cake Frosting

1	8-ounce package cream cheese
½	cup butter or margarine
1	box powdered sugar
1	teaspoon vanilla
1	cup chopped pecans

Cream cheese and butter. Add sugar, vanilla and pecans. Blend well. Add milk if necessary to spread.

This is Senator Bumpers' favorite cake, and Liza also made it for Chelsea Clinton's first three birthdays.

Liza with Governor Bumpers on Eliza Jane Ashley Day, December 20, 1974.

STATE OF ARKANSAS
EXECUTIVE DEPARTMENT

PROCLAMATION

TO ALL TO WHOM THESE PRESENTS SHALL COME--GREETINGS:

WHEREAS,   Eliza Jane Ashley has faithfully served the State of Arkansas through the administrations of four Governors and over a period of more than twenty years; and

WHEREAS,   Heads of State, visiting dignitaries from all over the world, and the citizens of Arkansas too numerous to categorize have enjoyed her cooking; and

WHEREAS,   Eliza Jane's talents are known far and wide and have been recognized by the media all across the state; and

WHEREAS,   Eliza Jane's abilities are unexcelled in any kitchen;

NOW, THEREFORE,   I, Dale Bumpers, Governor of Arkansas, do proclaim Friday, December 20, 1974

ELIZA JANE ASHLEY DAY

in the State of Arkansas and urge all Arkansans to pay tribute to her years of service to the first families of Arkansas.

IN WITNESS WHEREOF, I have hereunto set my hand and caused the Great Seal of the State of Arkansas to be affixed at Little Rock, the Capital, this nineteenth day of December, One Thousand Nine Hundred Seventy Four.

Dale Bumpers

GOVERNOR

Corned Beef Dinner

1	3-pound corned beef brisket
1	onion, chopped
2	garlic cloves, minced
2	bay leaves
6	small potatoes, pared
6	small carrots, pared
1	medium head cabbage, divided into 6 wedges

Place corned beef in Dutch oven; barely cover with hot water. Add onion, garlic and bay leaves. Cover; simmer about 3 hours or until tender.

Remove meat from liquid; add potatoes and carrots. Cover; bring to a boil; cook 10 minutes. Add cabbage and cook for 20 minutes more.

Carve meat across the grain, making thin slices.

Buttermilk Chicken

5	pounds cut-up chicken, washed and dried
1	cup buttermilk
1½	teaspoons salt
¼	teaspoon pepper
2	cloves garlic
2	tablespoons corn oil
1	cup chopped onion
2	tablespoons curry powder
	chopped almonds (optional)

Mix buttermilk, salt, pepper, garlic and corn oil. Marinate chicken in buttermilk mixture for 2 hours. Drain and save liquid.

Brown chicken lightly in hot oil. Add onion; saute slowly 10 minutes. Add curry powder. Add the almonds and reserved liquid. Cover; cook at 350° for 1 hour or until done.

This can be served with rice to give the meal an Indonesian flavor.

Stuffed Pork Chops

6	center-cut pork chops, about 1½ inches thick
2	cups cornbread, crumbled
1	cup light bread, crumbled
1	can chicken broth
1	teaspoon sage
½	teaspoon salt
2	eggs
	pepper to taste
½	cup diced celery
½	cup diced onion

Mix stuffing ingredients together and stuff in pork chops. Roll pork chops in flour and brown in skillet. Fasten with toothpicks. Bake in roasting pan covered at 350° for two hours or until done. During the last half hour of cooking time, uncover roasting pan and thicken broth for gravy.

Corn Pudding

1	16-ounce can corn
1	cup cream, seasoned with salt to taste
	pepper to taste
	nutmeg to taste
2	tablespoons melted butter
3	egg yolks, beaten
3	egg whites, stiffly beaten

Generously butter a baking dish. Mix above ingredients in order given, folding in egg whites last. Pour mixture in baking dish. Bake 35 to 40 minutes in 300° oven; raise heat to 375° and brown top for 10 to 15 minutes. Serve hot or cold.

Thumbprint Cookies

2	cups butter or oleo
1	cup brown sugar
4	eggs, separated
2	teaspoons vanilla
4	cups flour
1	teaspoon salt
2½	cups finely chopped nuts
1	jar fruit jelly

Mix butter, sugar, egg yolks and vanilla thoroughly. Sift flour and salt together and stir in. Roll into 1-inch balls. Dip balls into slightly beaten egg whites and roll in chopped nuts.

Place about 1 inch apart on ungreased baking sheets. Press thumb in center of each. Bake until set, about 8 minutes. Let cool. Place in print a bit of fruit jelly (or, for a change, try using powdered sugar tinted icing).

The nuts can be beat into the batter before the balls are rolled out.

Hot Rolls

¾	cup shortening
1	cup boiling water or scalded milk
2	eggs, beaten
¾	cup sugar
2	teaspoons salt
1	cup cold water
¼	cup lukewarm water
2	cakes yeast (or 2 packages dry yeast)
7½	cups sifted flour

Combine shortening and boiling water; stir until shortening is melted. Combine eggs, sugar and salt and beat in cold water. Soften yeast in ¼ cup lukewarm water. Combine the three mixtures and add flour. If dough is too soft to hold shape add ¼ cup more flour.

Cover and let stand in a warm (but not hot) place for two hours or until it doubles in bulk. Shape into rolls and allow to rise again until double in bulk. Bake at 400° for 20 to 30 minutes.

These rolls have been eaten by hundreds of people at the governor's table. One legislator used to come back to the kitchen and ask for the leftovers!

Crab Bisque

1	bunch green onions
1	pound lump crabmeat
½	cup butter
2	cans cream of mushroom soup
1	can cream of tomato soup
½	cup sherry
3	cups milk
3	tablespoons chopped parsley

Saute onion and crabmeat in butter. Add soups and blend. Add sherry, milk and parsley. Serve hot.

Yields 6 servings. Liza suggests accompanying this with spinach and hard rolls.

Swiss Steak

2½	pounds round steak, 1½ inches thick
½	cup flour
1	cup chopped onion
	salt, pepper and MSG to taste
1	can Del Monte Tomatoes
1	green pepper, cut in wedges
1	can mushrooms

Beat flour into steak. Brown onion in Crisco; add steak, salt, pepper and MSG. Top with tomatoes and peppers and cover with boiling water. Cover and simmer in oven 2 hours at 300°. Pour gravy into a separate bowl. To serve, put steak on platter and place mushrooms around the rim. Serve gravy on the side.

Liza says this simple dish is pretty enough for company.

Snickerdoodles

1	cup soft margarine
1½	cups sugar
2	eggs
2¾	cups flour
2	teaspoons cream of tartar
1	teaspoon baking soda
1	teaspoon salt
2	tablespoons sugar
2	teaspoons cinnamon

Mix margarine, sugar and eggs together well. Sift together flour, cream of tartar, baking soda and salt; stir into margarine mixture. Chill dough 20 minutes.

While dough is chilling, mix together the remaining 2 tablespoons sugar and the cinnamon. Roll dough into balls about the size of small walnuts; roll balls in cinnamon-sugar mixture.

Place about 2 inches apart on an ungreased baking sheet. Bake about seven minutes, or until slightly browned, at 400°.

Quick Aspic Salad

1½	cups V-8 cocktail vegetable juice
½	cup Hunt's tomato sauce
1	package lemon Jello
½	cup chopped celery
½	cup sliced stuffed olives
1	medium-sized avocado, diced
⅛	teaspoon grated onion (optional)
1	6½-ounce can Blue Plate shrimp, cleaned (optional)

Let V-8 and tomato sauce come to a boil. Dissolve lemon Jello in the hot mixture. Let cool and add other ingredients. Chill until set.

Raisin Pie

3	beaten eggs
1	cup sugar
½	teaspoon ground cinnamon
½	teaspoon ground nutmeg
¼	teaspoon salt
2½	tablespoons lemon juice
2	tablespoons butter or margarine, melted
1	cup raisins
⅓	cup broken walnuts
1	8-inch unbaked pie shell

Combine eggs, sugar, spices, salt, lemon juice and butter. Stir in raisins and nuts. Pour into pie shell. Bake in 375° oven for 35 to 40 minutes or until filling is set in center. Let cool before cutting.

Potato Rolls

2	yeast cakes (or 2 packages dry yeast)
1	cup warm water
¾	cup shortening
½	cup sugar
1	cup mashed potatoes
2	eggs, beaten
1	teaspoon salt
5½	cups flour
1	cup milk

Dissolve yeast in warm water and set aside. Cream shortening and sugar; add mashed potatoes and eggs. Sift flour with salt; alternately add flour and milk; add yeast. Mix thoroughly and refrigerate.

Take out 2 hours before baking. Bake at 400° until brown, 20 to 30 minutes.

These rolls are better made cloverleaf style in muffin tins, as the dough is very soft.

Governor and Mrs. Pryor pause on the Mansion's back steps with their sons, Scott, Mark and David, Jr. (Courtesy Office of Senator David Pryor)

Governor David Pryor
1975–1978

In January, 1975, Governor David Pryor, his wife, Barbara, and his sons — Dee, Mark and Scott — moved in the Mansion.

Mrs. Pryor liked to cook, so she had a lot of recipes and she was a great help in planning their menus. She told me what they liked and what they didn't like. Governor Pryor told me when he moved in to keep plenty of orange juice "but don't buy any Cokes or chewing gum for the boys." So we did just that. They liked Southern cooking, too. The boys liked lasagna and hamburgers. In fact, Governor Pryor had a burger that he called the Pryorburger, two patties that he grilled himself, with cheese and pickle relish in-between. The boys liked my chocolate chip cookies, too, so I made dozens of them.

He was a nice quiet man. He would get up and clear the table; he was about the only one who would. They had a house on the lake in Hot Springs and would spend a lot of weekends there. It was so funny to see the governor gather everything up and put it in a clothes basket and off they would go to Hot Springs.

We had three different secretaries while the Pryors were here — first Cissy McGuire and then Marilyn Blann and Peggy Simpson. My assistants were Rosie Spann, who cleaned the upstairs, and Emma Phillips, who cleaned the downstairs and helped in the kitchen.

The governor's mother, Miss Susie, used to come up from Camden and visit us all the time. She brought me lots of recipes, and she loved to cook. She was very religious and would come in the kitchen and discuss the Bible with me. She used to tell me that if she were younger she would get all my recipes and put them together for me, but she said she couldn't use her hands well enough to do it. One day I was talking to her, down in Camden, and I told her Mrs. Carolyn Huber had typed all my recipes for me and put them together. She was so happy that I had gotten them done. She said, "That's wonderful."

We had two famous visitors at the Mansion during those years, Colonel Sanders and Gregory Peck. Gregory Peck was here when the film *MacArthur* premiered in Little Rock. General MacArthur was born at the arsenal here. So Gregory Peck and his wife were entertained at a buffet here and spent the night in the guesthouse. He was so tall that the bed in the guesthouse was too short for him.

In 1976, Governor Pryor had the legislature change my title from "cook" to "food production manager."

In 1978, he was elected to the United States Senate and moved to Washington, D.C. He and Governor Bumpers are our two Senators now.

Pryorburger

For each Pryorburger, grill two hamburger patties outdoors. While patties are still warm, sandwich a slice of cheese and some pickle relish in-between. Serve with or without bun and dressings.

Lasagna

1	pound ground beef
2	tablespoons olive oil
1	medium onion, minced
1	clove garlic, chopped
1	tablespoon chopped parsley
2	6-ounce cans tomato paste
2	cups water
½	teaspoon salt
½	teaspoon pepper
1	8-ounce package lasagna noodles
2	eggs
¾	pound creamed cottage cheese
¾	pound mozzarella cheese, sliced
	grated Parmesan cheese

In a large heavy skillet, brown ground beef in olive oil with onion, garlic and parsley. Drain fat. Add tomato paste, 2 cups water, salt and pepper and simmer for 1 hour.

Cook lasagna noodles as directed on package. Mix eggs and cottage cheese together.

In 13" x 9" x 2" baking dish spread about ½ cup sauce, then alternate layers of lasagna, sauce, cottage cheese and egg mixture until baking dish is filled. Top with sauce and sprinkle with Parmesan cheese.

Bake at 375° for about 30 minutes or until heated through.

Yields 8 servings. This was a favorite of the Pryor boys.

Chicken Salad With Mandarin Oranges

2	whole chickens, boiled, chilled and diced
3	cups chopped celery
1	cup slivered almonds, toasted
	mayonnaise (enough to hold mixture together)
	juice of ½ lemon
	seasoning salt to taste
2	cans mandarin oranges, drained

Mix all ingredients together gently, adding mandarin oranges last. Toss lightly so as not to break oranges. Chill. Serve in lettuce cups.

Yields 12 servings.

Blueberry Torte

1	cup flour
½	cup chopped pecans
¼	cup brown sugar
½	cup butter
1	8-ounce package cream cheese
1	cup powdered sugar
1	teaspoon vanilla
2	packages dream whip
1	can blueberry pie filling

Mix flour, pecans, brown sugar and butter together. Pat into 9" x 13" pan. Bake at 400° for 15 minutes or until done.

Mix cheese, sugar and vanilla together. Beat dream whip by directions and mix into cheese. Pour into cooled crust. Spread top with fruit filling. Chill at least 8 hours or overnight.

This was served often at dinner parties during the Pryor administration.

Oven Chicken Parmesan

1	cut-up fryer or split chicken breasts
¼	cup flour
½	cup Parmesan cheese
2	teaspoons paprika
½	teaspoon salt
½	teaspoon pepper
½	cup butter or oleo, melted
1	egg, beaten
2	tablespoons milk

Mix flour, Parmesan cheese, paprika, salt and pepper. Dip chicken in egg and milk, then dredge in flour mixture. Place in shallow baking dish. Pour butter over chicken. Bake at 350° for 1¼ hours.

This was another favorite of the Pryor boys.

Chili Con Carne

1	pound ground beef
1	tablespoon butter
1	medium onion, chopped
1	#2 can Mexican-style beans
1	can cream of tomato soup
1	teaspoon salt
1	tablespoon chili powder

Brown beef in skillet with butter and onion. Add beans, soup, salt and chili powder. Simmer 1 hour.

This recipe was given to Liza by Barbara Pryor.

Susie's Charlotte Russe

1	envelope Knox gelatin
3	tablespoons cold water
1	cup milk
2	eggs, separated
2	tablespoons sugar
½	cup sugar
½	pint whipping cream
1	teaspoon vanilla
18	ladyfingers

Dissolve gelatin in cold water and set aside. Scald milk and add slowly to 2 beaten egg yolks. Beat in 2 tablespoons sugar and cook over hot water in double boiler until custard coats spoon. Remove from burner.

While mixture is hot, add gelatin solution. Let cool. Beat egg whites into stiff peaks; add egg whites and ½ cup sugar to custard. Whip cream and fold in; add vanilla and beat all together. Allow to harden.

Line pan with ladyfingers. Pour russe over them and serve.

This recipe was given to Liza by Governor Pryor's mother,
Miss Susie.

Tomato Bouillon

1	can cream of tomato soup
1	can beef bouillon
1	can water
	dash Worcestershire
	dash garlic salt
	dash celery salt

Combine soup, bouillon and water in saucepan and heat through. Season with Worcestershire, garlic salt and celery salt.

Ham Loaf

1½	pound uncooked cured ham
½	pound fresh lean pork
	milk
1	egg
3	tablespoons flour
1½	cups brown sugar
½	cup vinegar
½	cup water

Grind ham and pork and mix together well. Add enough milk to moisten. Add egg; beat all together and put in greased loaf pan.

Mix flour, brown sugar, vinegar and water. Pour over loaf. Bake at 350° for 1 hour.

Marinated Green Beans

3	cans whole green beans
1	cup salad oil
½	cup vinegar
½	cup sugar
4	buttons garlic
	salt, black pepper and red pepper to taste
1	jar pimentos

Put each garlic button on a toothpick and crush. Remove toothpicks. Rinse and drain beans. Mix oil, vinegar, sugar, garlic, salt and peppers and pour over drained beans. Cover and refrigerate overnight.

To serve, arrange individual servings of beans in bunches and top with a strip of pimento cut to resemble a bow.

Yields 9 servings.

Harlan Sanders, the originator of Kentucky Fried Chicken, with Liza and Willie Mae Rollins in the kitchen, 1977.

Curried Rice

4	cups long grain rice
2	teaspoons curry powder
2	tablespoons butter
4	cups chicken broth
1	jar green pimento olives
1	2½-ounce package slivered almonds

Combine rice, curry powder, butter and chicken broth, covered, in top of double boiler over boiling water (or cook as directed for rice). Cook until all moisture is absorbed and rice is tender and fluffy.

While rice is cooking, toast almonds and slice olives. When rice is cooked, add and toss almonds and olives. Refrigerate. Serve cold.

Yields 16 servings.

Heavenly Chocolate Pie

1	9-inch baked pie shell
2	eggs, separated
½	teaspoon vinegar
¼	teaspoon salt
½	teaspoon cinnamon, divided half and half
½	cup sugar
1	6-ounce package semi-sweet chocolate chips
3	tablespoons water
1	cup whipping cream
¼	cup sugar

Beat together egg whites, vinegar, salt, and ¼ teaspoon cinnamon until stiff but not dry. Gradually add sugar; beat until very stiff. Spread over bottom and sides of pie shell. Bake at 325° for 15 to 18 minutes. Cool.

Melt chocolate chips in top of double boiler over hot but not boiling water. Beat egg yolks with 3 tablespoons water and blend into chocolate. Stir until smooth. Spread 3 tablespoons of this chocolate mixture over cooled meringue in pie shell. Chill the remainder.

Whip cream until stiff. Add ¼ cup sugar and ¼ teaspoon cinnamon. Spread half of the cream over the chocolate layer in the pie shell. Fold reserved chocolate mixture into remaining whipped cream and spread over top of pie. Chill at least 4 hours.

Scotch Fudge

1	teaspoon soda
½	cup buttermilk
1	cup water
3	sticks butter or oleo
8	tablespoons cocoa
2	cups sugar
2	cups flour
2	eggs
½	teaspoon cinnamon
6	tablespoons milk
2	teaspoons vanilla
1	pound powdered sugar
¾	cup chopped pecans

Stir soda into buttermilk. Place water, 2 sticks butter and 4 tablespoons cocoa in a saucepan and bring to a boil.

While this is heating, mix sugar, flour, eggs, 1 teaspoon vanilla and cinnamon. After cocoa mixture comes to a boil, beat flour mixture into it. Pour into a jellyroll pan and bake for 20 to 30 minutes at 350°. It is done when it is no longer runny and pulls away from the sides of the pan.

While this is still warm and in the pan, melt 1 stick butter, 4 tablespoons cocoa and 6 tablespoons milk in a saucepan over low heat. Add 1 teaspoon vanilla and powdered sugar. Beat well until smooth. Stir in chopped pecans and pour over warm cake.

This was one of the Pryor boys' favorite desserts. Liza still makes it for birthdays and parties.

Broccoli Casserole

2	10-ounce packages broccoli spears
1	2½-ounce package slivered almonds
1	stick garlic cheese
1	can cream of mushroom soup
1	can cream of chicken soup

Cook broccoli in salted water. Drain and place in baking dish. Sprinkle with almonds. Slice garlic cheese and combine in saucepan with soups. Heat through until cheese is melted and pour over broccoli. Bake at 375° until bubbly.

Before serving, top with bread crumbs (cubed bread tossed in melted butter in skillet) and return to oven until crumbs are browned.

Yields 6 to 8 servings. Excellent for buffet dinner parties.

The Pryor family and Mansion staff treat Liza to a birthday party.

Orange Cake

1	cup shortening
2	cups sugar
4	eggs
1¼	cups buttermilk
1	teaspoon soda
3½	cups flour
⅛	teaspoon salt
2	teaspoons grated orange peel

Cream shortening and sugar well. Add eggs, one at a time, beating well after each. Measure buttermilk and add soda to it. Sift flour and salt together and add alternately with buttermilk to shortening mixture. Add orange peel.

Bake in tube pan at 325° for 40 to 50 minutes. Let cool, remove from tube pan and add frosting (recipe follows).

Orange Cake Frosting

1	cup orange juice
2	cups sugar
2	tablespoons grated orange peel

Mix together and bring to a boil. Pour over cake. The frosting will soak into cake.

This is Liza's son's favorite cake. She mails one to him in California every Christmas. She adds that it freezes well but suggests freezing it before wrapping it so the sauce won't stick to the wrapping.

Layer Salad

2½	cups chopped raw spinach
	salt, pepper and sugar to taste
1	pound crumbled, crisp bacon
4	eggs, hard-boiled and sliced
1	head finely chopped lettuce
1	cup frozen peas, uncooked
2	medium onions, sliced into rings
1	cup mayonnaise
1	cup Miracle Whip
	grated Swiss cheese

In 9" x 13" x 2" pan, layer spinach; salt, pepper and sugar; bacon; eggs; lettuce; salt, pepper and sugar; peas; and onion rings. Mix mayonnaise and Miracle Whip and spread over top. Sprinkle with grated Swiss cheese. Cover tightly and refrigerate for 24 hours.

Yields 6 to 8 servings. Liza often makes this for the governor and his family before leaving for the weekend.

Great Pickled Shrimp

3	pounds cooked shrimp
2	cups vinegar
10	bay leaves
1	pint Wesson oil
1	cup lemon juice
½	teaspoon red pepper
2	tablespoons salt
2	tablespoons paprika
1	teaspoon Tabasco
4	tablespoons catsup
6	medium onions, sliced into thin circles

Mix all ingredients except shrimp to make marinade. Add shrimp and marinate in refrigerator as long as possible — the longer the better.

Serve shrimp with toothpicks on the side.

After shrimp is served, the marinade can be reused for hard-boiled eggs.

After one of Liza's sumptuous dinners, Governor Pryor entertains his guests by playing his harmonica. Accompanying him on the guitar is Bill Worthen.

Governor Pryor with the Mansion staff: (from left) Ruby Davis, Liza, Floyd Sparks, the governor, Willie Mae Rollins and Calvin Shackleford. (Courtesy Governor's Office)

Liza and Governor Pryor test the fireplace in the Governor's Office at the State Capitol, c. 1977.

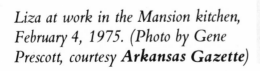

Liza at work in the Mansion kitchen, February 4, 1975. (Photo by Gene Prescott, courtesy **Arkansas Gazette**)

Governor Clinton holds the newborn Chelsea as Liza takes a peek.
(Photo by Donald R. Broyles, courtesy Governor's Office)

Governor Bill Clinton
1979–1980

In January, 1979, Governor Bill Clinton and his wife, Hillary, moved into the Mansion. This had me a little upset because he was only 32, the youngest governor I had every cooked for and I didn't know how we would get along. We soon became very good friends and like a family. They were like my children, since I was old enough to be their parent.

The governor and Miss Hillary liked different food to what the previous governors liked. They loved lamb, veal, fish, Mexican food. . .The governor loved pound cake and chess pie. Of course, they didn't want to eat too much because they were afraid they'd get fat. So we were on lots of diets. They also liked quiche.

Mrs. Carolyn Huber came to work as secretary for Miss Hillary, and she was a great help to all of us. Rosie Spann continued as the upstairs maid, and Emma was still downstairs and in the kitchen.

When the Clintons came they started honoring the valedictorians of all the high schools in Arkansas. The first party we had for them was in May, 1979. This was the first big crowd Miss Carolyn and I had to plan to feed. We cooked hams, turkeys, made chocolate chip cookies for several days before the day of the party. We were thrilled that over 1,000 students and their parents came. In the middle of the party we started running low on food and had to send out to the store to get more ham. This has been a tradition of honoring the valedictorians and salutatorians since then. We have always made sure we have enough food. Also, the Clintons opened up the Mansion more for

How to Broil Fish

If fish is frozen, allow to thaw completely. Wash fish in cold water; pat dry with a paper towel. Lightly brush broiler rack with salad oil. Arrange fish on rack and baste with one of the sauces below. Broil 4 inches from heat until fish flakes easily with fork but is still moist. Garnish with lemon wedges.

parties and charity fund raisers than had been done in the past.

We had the President's wife and the Vice President's wife come to visit us at different times in 1979 and 1980. Mrs. Rosalynn Carter was here for a function out in the backyard. This was all very exciting to us because we had to be cleared by the Secret Service before she came. They sent their team several weeks in advance to prepare for her visit. On the day of her arrival, the Secret Service came early that morning and stationed themselves all over the Mansion. She came into the Mansion, so everything upstairs where she was going to be for just a short time had to be cleared and checked by the Secret Service. She was a very delightful person.

Mrs. Joan Mondale also spent a night at the guesthouse in 1980. She was a very charming and down-to-earth person. She was in the state

campaigning, and she toured the Ozark Folk Center in Mountain View.

The Clintons did not have any children, and it had always been my dream to have a baby in the Mansion. One day I said to the governor, "It's time for you to have some children before you get too old." And he said, "If the Lord sees fit for us to, we will." Sure enough, after they were there a few months the governor and Miss Hillary told me they had something to tell me. They said, "We're going to have a baby in the Mansion." We were all on Cloud Nine.

Then on February 27, 1980, Chelsea Victoria Clinton was born. It was wonderful to have a baby come to the Mansion. I have never seen so many flowers and gifts that a baby got. I had always favored little boys, but when I saw Chelsea I loved her.

Marinated Chicken

10	pounds chicken drummettes (little drumsticks from wings)
1½	cups soy sauce
¾	cup dry sherry
1⅛	cups Hoysin Sauce
¾	cup plum jelly
18	green onions, minced
6	garlic cloves
¾	cup cider vinegar
½	cup honey

Combine all ingredients except chicken in saucepan. Bring to boil and simmer 5 minutes. Cool. Pour sauce over chicken, cover and refrigerate overnight.

Preheat oven to 375°. Place chicken on greased cookie sheets and bake uncovered for 1 to 1½ hours, basting frequently. Switch pans while cooking so that they cook evenly.

The Hoysin Sauce may take some hunting. Liza gets hers at Kim's Oriental Foods on University Avenue in Little Rock.

Sweet and Sour Carrots

2	pounds sliced carrots
1	bell pepper, diced
1	medium onion, diced
1	can tomato soup
½	cup oil
1	cup sugar
¾	cup vinegar
1	teaspoon prepared mustard
1	teaspoon Worcestershire sauce

Cook carrots until crispy tender. Drain off water. Toss with pepper and onion and set aside.

In saucepan, combine tomato soup, oil, sugar, vinegar, mustard and Worcestershire. Heat until boiling. Pour over carrots, pepper and onion and stir. Refrigerate at least 1 day.

This recipe is often served with the Hot Chicken Salad, which is found on the following page.

Hot Chicken Salad

2	cups chicken, cooked and cut up
2	cups celery, cubed and cooked until tender
2	cups rice, cooked in chicken broth
2	cans cream of chicken soup
1¼	cups mayonnaise
1	medium onion, chopped
6	tablespoons lemon juice
6	hard-boiled eggs, chopped
¾	cup slivered almonds
¼	cup butter, melted
1	cup crushed cornflakes

Prepare chicken, celery and rice. Combine cream of chicken soup, mayonnaise, onion, lemon juice and chopped eggs. Add first three ingredients and mix well. Place in casserole for baking.

Heat almonds in melted butter and pour on top of casserole. Top with cornflakes. Bake at 350° for 45 minutes.

Yields 12 to 16 servings. This is one of the first recipes a new governor has in the Mansion.

Key Lime Pie

1	9-inch baked pie shell
4	egg yolks
1	14-ounce can sweetened condensed milk
1	teaspoon grated lime peel
½	cup fresh lime juice
4	drops green food coloring (optional)
1	cup whipping cream, chilled
2	tablespoons confectioners' sugar
4	lime slices, halved

In medium mixing bowl, beat egg yolks until thick and lemon-colored, about 5 minutes. Add condensed milk, lime peel, lime juice, and food coloring, if desired. Beat until smooth.

Turn into pie shell, spreading evenly (filling will be soft). Cover with foil and refrigerate overnight.

Before serving, combine cream and confectioners' sugar in chilled mixing bowl; whip together until stiff. Spread evenly over pie. With fork, draw lines, and decorate with lime slices.

Bread Pudding

5	slices white bread
5	eggs
1	cup sugar
¼	cup butter or oleo, melted
2	cups milk
1	teaspoon vanilla
¼	teaspoon nutmeg
½	cup raisins (optional)

Remove crust from bread. Cut bread into cubes. Beat eggs; add sugar, butter, milk, vanilla and nutmeg.

Add bread and raisins if desired to mixture and mix well. Pour into greased 2-quart casserole and bake at 350° for 45 minutes.

This pudding cannot be served without its lemon sauce!

Lemon Sauce

1	cup sugar
1	tablespoon cornstarch
½	teaspoon salt
3	eggs, slightly beaten
	juice of 2 lemons
	rind of 2 lemons, grated
1	cup water
2	tablespoons butter

Mix sugar, cornstarch and salt. Add eggs, lemon juice, grated rind and water. Cook in double boiler until thick, stirring constantly. Add butter and let cool.

This sauce is also a necessity for Liza's rice and bread puddings.

Rice Pudding

2	cups rice, cooked
5	eggs
1	cup sugar
¼	cup butter or oleo, melted
2	cups milk
1	teaspoon vanilla
¼	teaspoon nutmeg
½	cup raisins (optional)

Beat eggs; add sugar, butter, milk, vanilla and nutmeg. Add rice and raisins if desired and pour into a greased 2-quart casserole. Bake at 350° for 45 minutes.

For a great topping, see the lemon sauce recipe that precedes this one.

Chicken and Rice

1	fryer, cut up
1	cup uncooked rice
2½	cups water
1	envelope Lipton's onion soup mix
	garlic salt
1	stick margarine

Grease 9" x 13" baking dish. Combine rice, water and soup mix and pour in baking dish. Sprinkle chicken with garlic salt and place on top of rice. Dot with margarine. Cook at 350° for 1½ hours.

Cold Steak Salad

2	pounds boneless sirloin, cut into ½-inch cubes
½	cup butter
¾	pound mushrooms, sliced
1	9-ounce package frozen artichoke hearts, cooked and cooled
1	cup finely diced celery
1	pint small cherry tomatoes
2	tablespoons chopped chives
2	tablespoons chopped parsley
2	cups salad dressing (recipe follows)
2	teaspoons Dijon mustard

In large skillet over high heat, saute meat in butter, a few cubes at a time until browned on all sides. Transfer to a large bowl and cool.

Quickly saute mushrooms in remaining butter and add to meat. Add artichoke hearts, celery, tomatoes, chives and parsley. Mix lightly.

Mix dressing with mustard. Pour over salad, toss, cover and marinate overnight.

This is one of Hillary Clinton's very favorite meals.

Italian Salad Dressing

2¼	cups oil
¾	cup wine vinegar
6	shallots, finely chopped
⅓	cup chopped parsley
⅓	cup fresh dill weed
	salt and freshly ground black pepper to taste
⅓	teaspoon Tabasco sauce

Combine all ingredients in a glass jar and shake.

Yields 3 cups.

Jello Pineapple 7-Up Salad

1	3-ounce package lime jello
1	15-ounce can crushed pineapple
8	ounces cream cheese
1	10-ounce bottle 7-Up
2	cups chopped nuts

Place jello mix, pineapple and cream cheese in saucepan over low fire; heat until jello dissolves, stirring constantly. Remove from fire and add 7-Up. Add chopped nuts. Pour into mold.

Using his own saxophone, Governor Clinton assists the Art Porter Trio in entertaining guests on the Mansion lawn. (Photo by Donald R. Broyles, courtesy Governor's Office)

Bran Muffins

2	cups boiling water
2	cups Kellogg's All-Bran Cereal
1	heaping cup Crisco
3	cups sugar
4	eggs
1	quart buttermilk
4	cups Nabisco 100% Bran Cereal
5	cups sifted flour
5	teaspoons soda
1	teaspoon salt

Pour boiling water over Kellogg's cereal. Let stand until cool. Cream Crisco and sugar. Add eggs, buttermilk and Nabisco cereal.

In a large container combine flour, soda and salt. Add to sugar mixture. Add Kellogg's cereal and mix until everything is moist. Bake at 400° for 15 to 20 minutes.

Yields 5 dozen muffins. Batter will keep for 6 weeks if kept covered in refrigerator.

Quiche Lorraine

1	9-inch unbaked pie shell
12	slices bacon, fried crisp and crumbled
1	cup shredded Swiss cheese
1/3	cup minced onion
4	eggs
2	cups whipping cream
3/4	teaspoon salt
1/8	teaspoon cayenne pepper

Preheat oven to 425°. Sprinkle bacon, cheese and onion into pie shell. Blend eggs, cream, salt and pepper and pour into shell. Bake 15 minutes or until knife inserted comes out clean.

Let stand 10 minutes before cutting and serving.

Liza serves this at small luncheons and suggests accompanying it with a tossed fresh vegetable salad and dry white wine.

Cheesecake

1	tablespoon butter
16	graham crackers, finely crushed
¼	cup sugar
16	ounces cream cheese, softened
3	eggs
⅔	cup sugar
¾	teaspoon vanilla
1	carton Smetina

Melt butter in 9-inch pan. Mix graham cracker crumbs and sugar and pat into pan to form crust.

When cream cheese is softened, mix in eggs one at a time and beat well. Add sugar and vanilla and beat at high speed with electric mixer until smooth. Spread filling over crust and bake at 275° for 30 to 35 minutes.

Top with Smetina and chill.

Mixed Vegetables Italienne

1	cup sliced carrots
¼	cup salad oil
1	pound stewed tomatoes
1	beef bouillon cube
4	cups cubed zucchini
1½	cups chopped green pepper
1	cup frozen peas
1	cup whole kernel corn
1	cup diced potatoes
1	cup coarsely chopped onion
1	teaspoon oregano
1½	teaspoons salt
⅛	teaspoon pepper

Cook carrots and drain. Pour oil into skillet. Add all other ingredients. Simmer for 20 to 25 minutes, stirring frequently.

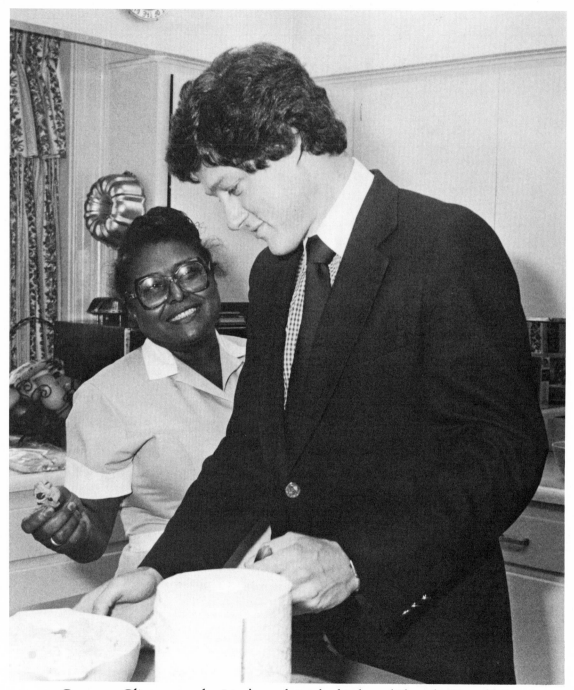

Governor Clinton samples Liza's work in the kitchen. (Photo by Donald R. Broyles, courtesy Governor's Office)

Governor and Mrs. Clinton and Zeke with Liza and other members of the Mansion staff, Christmas, 1979.

Governor and Mrs. White pose with Liza in the Mansion.

Governor Frank White
1981–1982

In January, 1981, Governor Frank White, his wife, Gay, and their children, Elizabeth, Rebecca and Kyle, came to live in the Mansion. Elizabeth was only here part-time because she was away in college in Illinois. This was the only governor that had his friends help him move in. Their friends did all the packing and unpacking for them, and all they had to do was come in the Mansion and go to bed.

Governor White loved to eat, too. He loved Mexican food, and after he moved here, Brownings' lost their trade. He would tell us what he wanted to eat on certain days. He would tell us when he was hungry for hot tamales and Mexican food, and some nights he would tell us to make the hamburger patties and leave them so he could grill them. Every Sunday he cooked steaks on the grill for his family and the troopers.

One of his favorite snacks was cheddar cheese and hot peppers. That man loved cheese, but he'd eat most anything. His favorite must have been chicken because Monday night was always chicken night. Mrs. White wasn't much of an eater, but she did like to cook. The children loved cookies, and I continued making my chocolate chip and butter cookies for them.

I liked the children. Sometimes Becky would come to me when her daddy wouldn't let her do something. I would have to tell her that I couldn't get into it!

They celebrated Christmas different from anyone I had ever seen. Everyone dressed in a costume from a different country. We cooked plum puddings and put money in them for gifts. Whoever cut the puddings would win the money.

Mrs. Gaye Lanford was the White's mansion administrator, and Becky Remmel helped out, too. Rosie and Emma continued as my two main assistants. I did all the cooking.

Two exciting things happened to me while the Whites were in the Mansion. One was when Mrs. Reagan was coming to Little Rock. Mrs. White invited me to go to the airport with her to meet Mrs. Reagan. I was thrilled to go. Then in October of 1982, the Whites gave me a surprise birthday party. Mrs. Bumpers, Mrs. Faubus and Governor and Mrs. Clinton all got to come. It was really a great day for me.

"One morning during our first week at the Mansion, I went downstairs to the kitchen to fix myself some breakfast. I reached for the oatmeal and a pan and had started to the stove when Liza asked me what I was doing. I said, 'Liza, I'm fixing some oatmeal.' To which she replied, 'Now, you let me do that for you. You might as well be Cinderella 'cause this ain't gonna last forever!'"

GAY WHITE

Kyle and Rebecca White campaigning for Dad! (Courtesy Mr. & Mrs. Frank White)

Gay White's Lasagna

1	pound sausage
½	pound hamburger
1	onion, chopped
1	green pepper, chopped
2	cloves garlic, crushed
1	tablespoon basil
2½	teaspoons salt
1	1-pound can whole tomatoes
12	ounces tomato paste
¾	cup red wine
2	teaspoons oregano
1	large carton large-curd cottage cheese
2	eggs, beaten
½	teaspoon pepper
1	tablespoon parsley
8	lasagna noodles, cooked and drained
12	ounces mozzarella cheese

Brown onion, green pepper and meat in large skillet. Drain off fat. Add garlic cloves, basil, 1½ teaspoons salt, tomatoes, tomato paste, red wine and oregano. Simmer uncovered for 1 hour, stirring occasionally.

Combine cottage cheese, eggs, 1 teaspoon salt, pepper and parsley. Set aside.

Place half of the cooked noodles in 13" x 9" x 2" pan. Spread half of the cottage cheese mixture over noodles; add half of the mozzarella cheese. Spread half the meat sauce over cheese. Repeat layers. Sprinkle parsley on top if you wish.

Bake at 375° for 45 minutes. Let stand 15 minutes before serving.

Yields 8 servings. Mrs. White says it's best to make this a day ahead to let flavors blend. Can be frozen.

Protein Health Salad

2	large butter lettuce heads
10	medium mushrooms
1	carrot, sliced
½	cup Spanish peanuts
3	tablespoons chopped parsley
2	tablespoons wheat germ, toasted
2	tablespoons sunflower seeds, toasted
2	tablespoons granola-type cereal
½	cup bean sprouts
½	cup shredded jack cheese
1	small avocado
2	hard-boiled eggs, quartered

Line a large serving bowl with outer lettuce leaves. Break remaining leaves into bite-size pieces. Place in bowl and mix with mushrooms, carrot and peanuts. Sprinkle in parsley, wheat germ, sunflower seeds, cereal, sprouts and cheese. Use your favorite salad dressing and garnish with sliced avocado and quartered eggs.

Yields 4 to 6 servings. This recipe was given to Liza by Gay White.

Taco Salad

1	pound lean ground beef
1	medium onion, chopped
1	15-ounce can kidney beans, drained
1½	teaspoons chili powder
½	teaspoon ground cumin
½	cup catsup or tomato sauce
2	medium avocadoes
1	medium head iceberg lettuce, shredded
1	cup shredded Cheddar or jack cheese
2	medium tomatoes, wedged
3	hard-boiled eggs, wedged
	tortilla chips
	sour cream
	red onion rings
	sliced ripe olives
	chopped green onion

Crumble beef in large skillet and cook over medium heat with onion. When meat has browned and onions are limp, drain and discard drippings. Add kidney beans, chili powder, cumin and catsup; stir and simmer over low heat about 5 minutes.

Peel, pit and slice avocadoes. Arrange lettuce on 4 dinner plates. Spoon beef mixture onto lettuce; top with cheese, tomato and egg wedges, avocado slices and tortilla chips.

Top salads with sour cream, onion rings, olives and green onion.

Yields 4 servings. This recipe was given to Liza by Gay White.

Company Punch

3	bananas
12	ounces frozen orange juice concentrate
12	ounces frozen lemonade concentrate
18	ounces pineapple juice
2	cups sugar
4	cups water
1½	gallons ginger ale

Combine bananas, orange juice and lemonade concentrates in blender or food processor. Heat sugar with water until sugar dissolves. Add to fruit juice mixture. Stir well and freeze in 2 ½-gallon milk carton containers.

An hour or two before serving, set cartons out to partially thaw. Place in punchbowl and add 3 quarts of ginger ale to each carton.

This recipe was given to Liza by Gay White.

Homemade Granola

2½	cups old-fashioned rolled oats
1	cup shredded coconut
½	cup coarsely-chopped almonds
½	cup sesame seeds
½	cup shelled sunflower seeds
½	cup wheat germ
½	cup honey
¼	cup cooking oil
½	cup chopped dried apricots
½	cup raisins

In large bowl, combine oats, coconut, almonds, sesame seeds, sunflower seeds and wheat germ. Combine honey and oil; stir into dry ingredients. Spread evenly in 13" x 9" x 2" pan. Bake at 300° until light golden brown for 45 to 50 minutes, stirring every 15 minutes.

Remove from oven; stir in apricots and raisins. Remove to another pan to cool. Stir occasionally during cooling to prevent lumping. When cold, store in tightly covered jars or plastic bags.

Yields 6½ cups.

Sunshine Sweet Potato Cups

8	large oranges
4	large sweet potatoes
1/3	cup butter or margarine, softened
1	8-ounce can crushed pineapple, drained
1/2	teaspoon salt
1/4	cup flaked coconut, toasted

slice for top of each orange; grate and save 2 teaspoons. Gently remove pulp, leaving shells intact. Set shells aside.

Cook sweet potatoes in boiling water 25 to 30 minutes or until tender. Let cool to touch; peel and mash.

Combine mashed potatoes, butter, pineapple, orange rind and salt; mix well. Spoon mixture into orange cups. Bake at 325° for 10 minutes. Before serving, sprinkle each cup with coconut.

Yields 8 servings. This was featured at several formal dinners hosted by the Whites.

Tex-Mex Dip

2	cans 10½-ounce bean dip
3	medium avocadoes, diced
2	tablespoons lemon juice
½	teaspoon salt
¼	teaspoon pepper
1	cup sour cream
½	cup mayonnaise
1	package taco seasoning mix
1	bunch green onions with tops, chopped
3	medium tomatoes, chopped
2	3½-ounce cans pitted ripe olives, sliced
8	ounces sharp cheddar cheese

Spread bean dip on large shallow serving platter. Mix avocadoes, lemon juice, salt and pepper. Spread over bean dip.

Mix sour cream, mayonnaise and taco seasoning mix. Spread over second layer. Sprinkle with chopped onions, tomatoes and olives. Cover with cheese.

Served chilled with large, round tortilla chips.

Overnight Layered Green Salad

1	medium head iceberg lettuce, shredded
½	cup thinly sliced green onion
1	cup thinly sliced celery
1	9-ounce can water chestnuts, drained and sliced
1	10-ounce package frozen peas
2	cups mayonnaise
2	teaspoons sugar
½	cup grated Parmesan cheese
1	teaspoon seasoned salt
½	teaspoon garlic powder
½	pound bacon, crisply cooked and crumbled
3	hard-boiled eggs, chopped
2	medium tomatoes, wedged

In a 3- or 4-quart shallow glass serving bowl, make a layer of shredded lettuce. Top with consecutive layers of onion, celery, water chestnuts and frozen peas. Spread evenly with mayonnaise. Sprinkle with sugar, cheese, salt and garlic powder. Cover and refrigerate for several hours or overnight.

Before serving, crumble bacon into salad. Sprinkle with chopped eggs. Arrange tomato wedges around salad.

To serve, use a spoon and fork to lift out each serving, which should include some of each layer.

Yields 8 to 10 servings. This recipe was given to Liza by Gay White.

King Ranch Chicken

1	3-pound hen
2	onions (1 whole and 1 chopped)
1	rib celery
	salt and pepper to taste
1	large bell pepper, chopped
1	can cream of mushroom soup
1	can cream of chicken soup
½	pound Cheddar cheese, grated
	chili powder
	garlic salt
1	package frozen tortillas
1	can Rotel Tomatoes and Chilies, drained

Boil hen until tender in water seasoned with whole onion, celery, salt and pepper. Cut chicken into bite-size pieces and reserve all stock. Combine soups and grate cheese.

Just before putting casserole together, soak frozen tortillas in boiling chicken stock until they wilt. Layer 9" x 13" baking dish with tortillas (with plenty of stock), chicken, chopped onion, bell pepper, chili powder, garlic salt, soup mixture and cheese. Repeat the layers.

Cover casserole with Rotel tomatoes and chilies and reserved stock until juices are about half the depth of the dish. Refrigerate overnight.

Bake uncovered at 375° for 30 minutes.

Yields 8 servings. This recipe was given to Liza by Gay White.

Governor and Mrs. White with their children, Kyle, Rebecca and Elizabeth, Christmas 1981. (Courtesy Mr. & Mrs. Frank White)

Italian Salad

1	20-ounce package frozen broccoli, thawed
2	small cans mushrooms
1	can water chestnuts
1	can black olives
4	stalks celery, chopped
	green pepper strips
4	green onions, chopped
1	small bottle Italian salad dressing
	cherry tomatoes

Slice mushrooms and water chestnuts. Cut black olives in half. Chop celery and green onions.

Combine vegetables in flat pan. Pour dressing over mixed vegetables. Marinate, stirring occasionally, for at least 8 hours.

Before serving, garnish with cherry tomato halves.

This was one of the Whites' favorite recipes, and Liza served it often for them and their guests.

Soda Cracker Pie

3	egg whites
¼	teaspoon cream of tartar
1	cup sugar
36	soda crackers, crushed
1	cup chopped pecans
1	teaspoon vanilla
1	cup whipping cream
4	tablespoons apricot preserves

Beat egg whites until foamy. Add cream of tartar. Beat until stiff but not dry. Gradually add sugar; whip until glossy.

Combine soda cracker crumbs and chopped pecans; add vanilla. Fold in egg whites. Mix well and pour into greased glass pie plate or 9-inch square Pyrex dish.

Bake at 350° until firm, about 20 minutes. **Do not overcook.**

Whip cream and fold in apricot preserves. Spread on top.

Liza says you can substitute crushed, drained pineapple for the preserves for a change.

Canadian Cheese Soup

1	stick oleo
¼	cup minced onion
½	stalk celery, finely chopped
¼	cup grated carrots
½	cup flour
2	tablespoons cornstarch
2	cups chicken stock
1	quart milk
2	cups Velveeta cheese, grated

Saute onion, celery and carrot in oleo. Cream flour and cornstarch; add chicken stock and milk. Cook until thick. Add sauteed ingredients and cheese. Cover and simmer 1 hour.

Chess Cake

1	box lemon cake mix
3	eggs
½	cup butter, melted
8	ounces cream cheese
1	box powdered sugar
1	teaspoon vanilla

Mix lemon cake mix, 1 egg and butter. Press in bottom of 9" x 12" pan. Mix cream cheese, 2 eggs, powdered sugar and vanilla; spread over bottom layer. Bake at 350° for 45 to 50 minutes.

Liza with Governor White and former Governor Faubus.

Mrs. White supervises work in the Mansion vegetable garden. On hand to assist are Willie Benton (left), Johnny Bopp and the Whites' dog, Vicki.

Governor Clinton, Mrs. Clinton and their daughter, Chelsea, Christmas, 1983.

Governor Bill Clinton
1983–Present

In January, 1983, Governor Bill Clinton, his wife, Hillary, and little Chelsea moved back to the Mansion. I was thrilled to have them back again and to see Chelsea. Chelsea has grown into a little lady now and keeps us all hopping. We are having a wonderful time. One day Chelsea told me she didn't have a great-grandmother, so, she said, since I was the oldest thing here at the Mansion, I was going to be her great-grandmother. We had a big laugh over this.

Since Chelsea has been back at the Mansion we have all enjoyed celebrating her birthday. She loves to blow out the candles and she always has me make a carrot cake for her birthday.

Chelsea is really growing up now and attends pre-school and will be going to kindergarten next year. Her favorite dish is macaroni and cheese and fried chicken legs and ham.

This is the first governor we have had where both he and his wife get up and go to work every morning. Miss Hillary has a lot of really good help now. Robyn Dickey is the mansion administrator and Becky McCoy is her assistant. Kim Bellingrath helped out for a while, too. Virginia Pennington helps in the kitchen.

The Clintons still like to eat but keep on diets most of the time. He really likes Mexican food, especially my chicken enchiladas. Now the governor has won another election and will be here for another two years. I am looking forward to that.

Pudding Cake Dessert

1	stick butter, softened
1	cup flour
1	cup chopped pecans
8	ounces cream cheese
1	cup powdered sugar
1	large container Cool Whip, thawed
1	4½-ounce package instant chocolate pudding
1	3¾-ounce package instant French vanilla pudding
2	cups cold milk
	grated chocolate

Combine butter, flour and pecans. Press into 13" x 9" x 2" pan and bake at 350° for 20 minutes. Cool.

Blend cream cheese, powdered sugar and 1 cup Cool Whip. Spread over cooled crust.

Blend instant puddings with milk until thick. Spread over cream cheese filling. Top with remaining Cool Whip. Grate chocolate over top if desired. Chill well.

Liza served this to the Ozark Committee of 100 and everyone wanted the recipe, so here it is. This recipe can incorporate any flavors of pudding. An alternate method of preparing is to mix the puddings separately so that there are two layers of pudding.

Veal Marsala

1½	pounds veal scallopini
¾	tablespoons salad oil
	flour
	paprika
⅔	tablespoon butter
½	pound sliced mushrooms
2	tablespoons chopped chives
2	tablespoons chopped parsley
	salt and pepper to taste
1½	cups beef broth
½	cup Marsala wine

Heat oil in skillet. Dust veal slices lightly in flour and saute a few slices at a time quickly over high heat until browned. Transfer slices to a baking dish and sprinkle each slice with paprika.

Melt butter in skillet. Add mushrooms and saute about 5 minutes. Add chives, parsley, salt, pepper, beef broth and wine. Simmer 5 minutes. Pour sauce over veal slices in baking dish and bake at 350° for 30 minutes.

Yields 4 to 6 servings. Liza recommends serving this over noodles.

Cauliflower with Shrimp Sauce

1	large head cauliflower
8	ounces frozen shrimp
1	can Campbell's shrimp soup
1	cup sour cream
	milk
1	cup slivered almonds, toasted

Separate cauliflower into flowerets. Cook in boiling water until tender. Drain and set aside. Cook frozen shrimp briefly. Cut into chunks and set aside.

Blend together soup, sour cream and enough milk to make a good, thick, pourable sauce. Heat well and add shrimp, heating through. **Do not boil.**

If cauliflower was prepared early in the day, reheat and redrain. Place in serving bowl and top with shrimp sauce. Sprinkle with toasted almonds.

Shrimp Gumbo

3	strips bacon, cut in small pieces
1	onion, minced
1	bell pepper, minced
1	pod garlic, crushed
1	cup celery tops
1	can consomme
1	can whole tomatoes
	salt and pepper to taste
1	pound frozen shrimp, de-veined

Put everything in boiler except shrimp. Cook slowly for about 2 hours. Add shrimp and cook another 30 minutes. If it gets too thick, add a little water.

Eagle Brand Lemon Pie

1	9-inch baked pastry shell
3	eggs, separated
1	14-ounce can Eagle brand milk
½	cup lemon juice
4	drops yellow food coloring (optional)
¼	teaspoon cream of tartar
⅓	cup sugar

*The Clintons prefer whipped cream to meringue on this pie. I use two cups of whipping cream and leave out the egg whites, cream of tartar and sugar.

Preheat oven to 350°. In medium bowl, beat egg yolks and stir in milk, lemon juice, and food coloring if desired. Pour into pastry shell.

In small bowl, beat egg whites with cream of tartar until soft peaks form, gradually adding sugar. Beat until stiff but not dry. Spread this meringue on top of pie, sealing carefully to edge of shell.

Bake 12 to 15 minutes or until meringue is golden brown. Cool and chill until serving time.

This pie is a favorite of Governor Clinton's mother.

Black Bean Soup

2	cups dried black beans
¼	cup butter
2	stalks celery, chopped
1	medium onion, chopped
1	tablespoon all-purpose flour
¼	cup chopped parsley
	rind and bone from a smoked ham
2	bay leaves
1½	teaspoons salt
¼	teaspoon pepper
½	cup dry madeira
2	tablespoons vinegar

Pick over and wash the beans. Cover them with water and soak overnight. Drain the beans, then add 8 cups of cold water. Cover and simmer for 1½ hours.

Melt the butter in a heavy pot. Add celery and onion and saute until tender but not brown. Blend in the flour and stir for 1 minute. Add parsley, beans and cooking liquid, ham rind and bone, bay leaves, salt and pepper. Cover and simmer for 3 hours.

Discard the ham bone and rind but retain any bits of meat. Put the soup through a sieve or puree in an electric blender. Add wine and vinegar. Reheat the soup and serve.

Oatmeal Cookies

1¼	cup unsifted all-purpose flour
1	teaspoon baking soda
1	cup butter, softened
¼	cup granulated sugar
¾	cup light brown sugar, firmly packed
1	package (4-serving size) Jello vanilla instant pudding
2	eggs
3½	cups quick-cook rolled oats
1	cup raisins (optional)

Mix flour with baking soda. Combine butter, sugars and pudding mix in large mixer bowl; beat until smooth and creamy. Beat in eggs.

Gradually add flour mixture; then stir in oats and raisins. Batter will be stiff.

Drop by rounded teaspoons onto ungreased baking sheets, about 2 inches apart. Bake at 375° for 10 to 12 minutes.

Yields 5 dozen cookies.

A Trilogy of Fish Sauces

CURRY SAUCE

2	tablespoons salad oil
2	tablespoons lemon juice
¼	teaspoon curry powder

LEMON SAUCE

3	tablespoons lemon juice
⅛	teaspoon dry mustard
1	bay leaf, crumbled

HERBED SAUCE

2	tablespoons salad oil
2	tablespoons lemon juice
¼	teaspoon paprika
¼	teaspoon basil

(From left) Rosie Spann, Liza, Emma Phillips and Carolyn Huber pitch in on kitchen chores. (Photo by Donald R. Broyles, courtesy Governor's Office)

Lemony Steamed Fish

6	fish fillets
1	small onion, finely chopped
⅓	cup chopped parsley
1½	teaspoons dill weed
1½	teaspoons paprika
½	teaspoon salt
½	teaspoon pepper
3	teaspoons lemon juice

Center each fillet on a 12-inch square of foil. Sprinkle with onion, parsley, dill weed, paprika, salt, pepper and lemon juice.

Fold foil over each fillet to make a pocket; pleat seams to enclose securely and place on cookie sheet. Bake at 375° for 30 minutes.

Yields 6 servings.

Poppy Seed Dressing

1½	cups sugar
2	teaspoons salt
2	teaspoons dry mustard
⅔	cup vinegar
3	tablespoons onion juice
2	cups salad oil
3	tablespoons poppy seeds

Mix sugar, salt, mustard and vinegar. Add onion juice and stir thoroughly. Add oil slowly, beating constantly until thick. Add poppy seeds and beat for a few minutes. Refrigerate.

The Clintons eat lots of fruit salad in the summer, so Liza always has this dressing in the refrigerator for them.

Chicken Enchiladas

	cooking oil
2	4-ounce cans green chilies
1	large clove garlic, minced
1	28-ounce can tomatoes
2	cups chopped onion
2	teaspoons salt
½	teaspoon oregano
3	cups shredded, cooked chicken
2	cups dairy sour cream
2	cups grated Cheddar cheese
15	corn tortillas

Preheat oil in skillet. Chop chilies after removing seeds; saute with minced garlic in oil.

Drain and break up tomatoes; reserve ½ cup liquid. To chilies and garlic add tomatoes, onion, 1 teaspoon salt, oregano and reserved tomato liquid. Simmer uncovered until thick, about 30 minutes. Remove from skillet and set aside.

Combine chicken with sour cream, grated cheese and other teaspoon salt. Heat ⅓ cup oil; dip tortillas in oil until they become limp. Drain well on paper towels.

Fill tortillas with chicken mixture; roll up and arrange side by side, seam down, in 9" x 13" x 2" baking dish. Pour chili sauce over enchiladas and bake at 250° until heated through, about 20 mintues.

Yields 15 enchiladas. This is Governor Clinton's favorite Mexican dish.

Lemon Chess Pie

1	9-inch unbaked pie shell
2	cups sugar
½	cup butter or margarine
5	eggs
1	cup milk
1	tablespoon flour
1	tablespoon cornmeal
¼	cup fresh lemon juice
	rind of 3 lemons, grated

Cream sugar and butter; add eggs and milk. Beat well. Then add flour, cornmeal, lemon juice and lemon rind.

Pour mixture into pie shell; bake at 350° until done, 35 to 40 minutes.

Governor Clinton likes a lot of pies, but this is his absolute favorite.

Banana Muffins

½	cup butter
1½	cups sugar
2	eggs, well-beaten
1	teaspoon soda
2	cups flour
½	cup buttermilk
3	bananas, mashed
½	cup chopped nuts

Cream butter and sugar. Add eggs. Mix soda with flour; alternating with buttermilk, add gradually to butter mixture. Add bananas and nuts. Bake at 350° for 20 to 25 minutes.

Yields 2 dozen muffins. This is a favorite of Roger Clinton's.

Butter Babies

2	cups Bisquick
1	cup heavy cream
½	stick butter

Combine Bisquick and cream, stirring until well mixed. Turn dough onto surface sprinkled lightly with Bisquick and pat out to ½" thickness. Dough will be sticky. Cut with 1" round cutter.

Melt butter in pan with sides in 350° oven. Dip each biscuit (both sides) into butter and bake at 350° for about 15 minutes.

This recipe was served at the Legislative Spouse Luncheon on February 21, 1983.

Beef Tenders

6	pounds beef tenders
1	16-ounce bottle Wishbone Italian salad dressing
	coarse black pepper to taste

Marinate meat in salad dressing for 4 to 5 hours, turning periodically. Sprinkle with coarse black pepper. Then grill on barbecue grill to desired doneness. This will melt in your mouth.

This is Governor Clinton's favorite meat. Liza serves it often at formal dinners.

Sweet and Sour Slaw

3	pounds cabbage, grated
1	medium onion, chopped
1	green pepper, chopped
1	cup sugar
¾	cup oil
¾	cup vinegar
1½	teaspoons salt
1	teaspoon celery seed
1	teaspoon dry mustard

Combine cabbage, onion and green pepper. Pour sugar over vegetables.

In saucepan, combine oil, vinegar, salt, celery seed and mustard; heat to boiling. Pour over slaw and stir. Refrigerate overnight.

This recipe makes enough slaw to last a family a week.

Chelsea Clinton looks up to Joe Klein.

Mrs. Clinton addresses the Arkansas General Assembly in support of her husband's education program for the state. (Courtesy Old State House Museum)

*Liza takes a shift at the silver punchbowl from the **U.S.S. Arkansas**.*

Recipes for Holidays and Receptions

In her thirty years at the Mansion, probably half of the cooking Liza has done has been for large crowds invited to teas and receptions by the governors and their families. This cookbook wouldn't be complete without our asking her to divulge the recipes for some of her most-often-served appetizers, dips and holiday foods.
— Ed.

Stained Glass Windows

1	12-ounce package semi-sweet chocolate drops
½	cup butter or oleo
1	6-ounce package colored marshmallows
½	cup finely chopped pecans
1	package shredded coconut

Melt chocolate drops and butter in top of double boiler; let cool. Add marshmallows and nuts. Form into logs and roll in coconut. Refrigerate.

Cut into ¼-inch slices when ready to serve.

These are a beautiful addition to a Christmas reception.

Cheese Wafers

½	cup butter
1	cup grated sharp Cheddar cheese
1	cup flour
1	cup Rice Krispies
4	hard shakes Tabasco sauce

Mix and form into balls; mash tops with fork. Bake at 400° for 10 minutes.

Cocoons

½	cup butter or margarine
¼	cup confectioner's sugar
½	teaspoon vanilla
1	cup chopped nuts
1	cup all-purpose flour

Cream butter with sugar and vanilla until light and fluffy. Add ½ cup nuts and stir. Blend flour and remaining nuts and add to mix. Shape like cocoons on ungreased cookie sheets. Bake at 325° for 20 minutes. When cool, roll in confectioner's sugar.

Yields 32 cocoons.

Spinach Dip

1	10-ounce package chopped frozen spinach
1	can water chestnuts
2	cups sour cream
3	tablespoons mayonnaise
1	package dry Knorr's vegetable soup mix
3	green onions, finely chopped

Thaw and drain spinach. Drain water chestnuts and chop coarsely. Mix all ingredients and chill.

Liza recommends serving Triscuits with this dip.

Sausage Balls

2½	cups Bisquick
1	cup Cheddar cheese, grated
1	pound sausage

Mix all ingredients together. Roll into balls about 1 inch in diameter. Bake for 15 minutes, or until brown, at 400°.

Yields 50 sausage balls. These may be frozen before baking;
however, Liza says baking will probably take another 10 minutes or so.

Rolled Asparagus Sandwiches

1	loaf thin-sliced sandwich bread
2	cans whole asparagus
	soft butter
	Parmesan cheese
	paprika

Trim crusts off bread. Drain asparagus and pat dry. Spread each slice of bread with softened butter. Place one spear asparagus on each slice of bread and roll up. Spread a little butter on top of each sandwich. Sprinkle with Parmesan cheese and paprika. Bake at 350° until slightly toasted, about 15 minutes.

Chutney Cheese Pate

16	ounces cream cheese
2	cups shredded sharp Cheddar cheese
1	jar Kraft Old English Cheese
3	tablespoons sherry or vermouth
1	teaspoon curry powder
½	teaspoon salt
1½	8-ounce jars Major Grey's Mango Chutney
	green onion tops, finely sliced

Beat together at room temperature cheeses, sherry, curry powder and salt. Spread on serving platter, shaping a layer about ½-inch thick. Spread chutney thickly on top, almost to cover. Before serving, sprinkle with green onions.

Yields appetizer for 16 to 20. Liza recommends serving it with Escort crackers.

Cucumber Sandwiches

1	loaf thinly sliced white bread
8	ounces cream cheese
1	large cucumber, grated
1	small onion, grated
1	cup mayonnaise

Remove crusts from bread. Mix cream cheese, cucumber, onion and mayonnaise. Spread onto bread to make sandwiches. Quarter sandwiches into small triangles and serve.

Lemon Squares

2	sticks butter, softened
2	cups flour
½	cup powdered sugar
4	eggs
2	cups sugar
6	tablespoons lemon juice
1	tablespoon flour
½	teaspoon baking powder

Mix butter, flour and powdered sugar and press into 10" x 14" pan. Bake at 325° for 15 minutes.

Beat eggs slightly. Add sugar, lemon juice, flour and baking powder. Mix and pour on top of pastry. Bake at 325° for 40 to 50 minutes.

Upon removing from oven, sprinkle with additional powdered sugar. Cool and cut into squares.

Crunchy Frozen Punch

3	3-ounce packages gelatin (any flavor)
9	cups boiling water
4	cups sugar
4	cups water
1	16-ounce bottle lemon juice
2	46-ounce cans pineapple juice
6	quarts ginger ale

Dissolve gelatin in boiling water. Combine sugar with 4 cups water and bring to a quick boil. Add to gelatin mixture and set aside to cool.

Add lemon juice and pineapple juice. Mix well and freeze in a plastic bucket covered with foil.

When ready to serve, put in a large container and add ginger ale to consistency desired. This punch may be broken up with a large knife as it thaws. It is ready to serve when it is slushy.

Yields 50 servings. This punch is featured in the Mansion at Christmas parties.

Broccoli Dip

3	stalks celery, chopped
½	large onion, minced
1	can mushrooms
1	10-ounce package frozen broccoli, cooked
1	roll garlic cheese
1	can cream of mushroom soup

Saute celery and onion in butter. Add soup and cheese. Drain broccoli and add in all other ingredients. Mix well and serve.

Avocado Dip

8	ounces cream cheese
1	cup mashed avocado
3	tablespoons lemon juice
3	dashes Worcestershire sauce
3	dashes Tabasco sauce
⅓	cup finely chopped green onion
1	teaspoon salt

Add avocado slowly to cream cheese, blending until smooth. Add lemon juice, Worcestershire sauce, Tabasco sauce, onions and salt and mix thoroughly. Place in bowl on tray, surrounding with Fritos.

Spinach Balls

1	10-ounce package frozen chopped spinach, cooked
1	large onion, minced
1	small package herbed seasoned stuffing mix
5	eggs
¾	cup melted butter
½	cup Parmesan cheese
1	tablespoon garlic salt
½	teaspoon pepper
1	teaspoon thyme

Drain spinach. Saute onion in a little extra butter until clear. Mix all ingredients and chill. Roll into small balls for hors d'oeuvres. Bake 10 minutes at 350°.

Yields 75 spinach balls. These can be frozen.

Sandies

1	cup butter
¼	cup confectioner's sugar
2	teaspoons vanilla
1	tablespoon water
2	cups flour
1	cup chopped nuts

Cream butter and confectioner's sugar; add vanilla and water. Add flour; mix well and stir in nuts.

Shape batter into small rolls 1½ inches long. Bake on ungreased cookie sheet at 300° for 20 minutes or until golden brown.

While hot, roll in confectioner's sugar.

Drop Butter Cookies

1	cup butter
1	cup sugar
¼	teaspoon salt
1	egg
1	teaspoon vanilla
2	cups flour

Cream butter, sugar and salt. Add egg, vanilla and flour and beat well. Drop by the half-teaspoonful on greased or Teflon cookie sheet. Bake about 10 minutes, or until edges brown, at 350°.

Besides being a standby for teas and receptions, these have been popular among the children who have lived in the Mansion.

Dill Weed Dip

⅔	cup mayonnaise
⅔	cup sour cream
1	tablespoon grated onion
1	teaspoon Beau Monde seasoning
1	teaspoon dill weed
1	teaspoon parsley flakes

Mix ingredients and refrigerate overnight.

Liza suggests serving this dip in the center of hollowed-out pumpernickel bread. Great with vegetables!

Apricot Balls

1	can Eagle brand milk
1	pound ground apricots
3	cups coconut
	powdered sugar

Mix milk, apricots and coconut. Roll into balls about 1 inch in diameter. Roll in powdered sugar. Let dry completely before storing in tight container.

Liza says that for a change you can decrease coconut and add nuts or dates.

Greek Crescents

1	cup butter
¾	cup sugar
1	egg yolk
2	tablespoons brandy
2½	cups sifted flour
½	teaspoon baking powder
½	cup chopped pecans
	confectioner's sugar

Beat butter with electric mixer until light and fluffy. Add sugar gradually and mix well. Beat in egg and brandy.

Sift together flour and baking powder and mix into butter mixture with wooden spoon. Stir in nuts.

Turn batter out on a lightly floured board and knead gently about 2 minutes. Using a tablespoon, shape into crescents. Place on ungreased cookie sheet and bake at 375° for 25 minutes.

Cool slightly and sprinkle with confectioner's sugar.

Yields 3 dozen cookies.

Frozen Lemon Cream

10	lemons
5	cups milk
5	cups sugar
5	cups heavy cream, unwhipped
1	pinch salt
2½	teaspoons lemon extract

Extract juice from lemons and reserve. Grate rind and reserve.

Combine milk, sugar, cream and salt in saucepan and heat just until sugar is dissolved. Be careful not to let mixture boil. Pour into freezing tray and freeze until firm.

When frozen, spoon into large bowl and beat with electric mixer for a few minutes, adding lemon rind, lemon juice and lemon extract. When mixture is smooth and creamy, return to tray. While mixture is still mushy, beat with a fork until smooth. Continue freezing until firm.

Yields 30 servings.

Party-Size Apple Pies

1	8-ounce package dried apples
1	cup oleo, softened
6	ounces cream cheese
2½	cups flour
1	teaspoon salt

Cook dried apples according to instructions on package. Combine oleo, cream cheese, flour and salt to make dough. Roll out very thin and cut with a glass (diameter 2⅝ inches); put ½ teaspoon apple mixture in each pastry circle.

Fold pastries over and crimp with fork. Stick fork in dough to make air holes. Bake at 350° for 25 minutes.

These are often served at Christmas parties at the Mansion.

Index

IF YOU HAVE ENJOYED THIS FINE BOOK,

Send for the complete August House Catalog
of Arkansas books. Please enclose $2 to
defray delivery costs.

August House, Inc., Publishers
Post Office Box 3223
Little Rock, Arkansas 72203-3223